TEACHING
CRITICAL THINKING

TEACHING ———— CRITICAL THINKING

Grace E. Grant

PRAEGER

New York
Westport, Connecticut
London

Library of Congress Cataloging-in-Publication Data

Grant, Grace E.
    Teaching critical thinking.

    Bibliography: p.
    Includes index.
    1. Critical thinking—Study and teaching (Secondary)
I. Title.
BF441.G73   1988   153.4'3'07   87-29289
ISBN 0-275-92749-0 (alk. paper)

Library of Congress Catalog Card Number: 87-29289
ISBN: 0-275-92749-0

First published in 1988

Praeger Publishers, One Madison Avenue, New York, NY 10010
A division of Greenwood Press, Inc.

Printed in the United States of America

The paper used in this book complies with the Permanent
Paper Standard issued by the National Information Standards
Organization (Z39.48–1984).

10 9 8 7 6 5 4 3 2 1

For Dennis

Contents

Figures

Acknowledgments

In any ambitious research project such as this one, there are inevitably many whose help was crucial and many to thank. James England, then of Occidental College, encouraged a fleeting idea in 1984 that led to the formulation of this project, and David Danelski motivated the difficult early stages of this analysis. Further support came from a John D. MacArthur Research Professorship at Occidental, which permitted the time for long-term observational research.

The four teachers who allowed me into their classrooms and talked to me so freely during the course of this study are very much a part of the authorship of this book. Their words appear in almost every chapter. They made me think about teaching critical thinking in ways I had not thought before and called my attention to influencing factors that I had overlooked. Throughout the analysis of their work, I have continued to admire and respect their dedication, excellence, and professionalism as teachers.

Many other colleagues and friends have provided particular references as well as general encouragement. Those who read the manuscript in whole or in part were: Frances Klein, Charles Kerchner, Rae McCormick, and Dennis Tierney. I am grateful for their reactions and suggestions even when I did not heed them. Individual chapters were read by Jere Brophy, Carolyn Ellner, Sharon Feiman-Nemser, Judy Grayson, John Olson, Virginia Richardson-Koehler, and Anna Richert. Their questions and doubts prodded me toward greater clarity. Syd Brown gave valuable assistance on the figures; and Jane Rankin contributed through her editing and many other forms of support.

Introduction: Teaching Critical Thinking

How do secondary teachers develop students' ability to reason? How do their conceptions of subject matter shape thinking about these goals? How do they transform these conceptions into instructional processes—presenting information, designing work tasks for students, and maintaining student involvement in these tasks? These questions are highlighted in recent national debates over excellence in secondary schooling and excellence in teaching.

Through the work of four experienced high school teachers—Bob Post, Langdon Selhorst, Linda Reed, and Conrad Rizzo*—we can begin to understand the teacher knowledge necessary to teach students to reason about history, government, literature, and physics. These four teachers speak of their chosen goals, of their choice of activities to reach those goals, and of their difficulties of working with students in groups. Their statements reveal a conception of content that influences these choices. Bob focuses attention upon the social impact of historical events, Langdon upon the differences between parliamentary and republican democracies, Linda upon the psychological relationships and sibling rivalry in *King Lear*, and Conrad upon the physical properties of light. The four also speak of individual students, of past influences on their teaching, and of past successes and failures. In transforming these concepts into instructional activities, each emphasizes reading critically, writing with clarity, predicting outcomes accurately, and thinking independently.

The four teachers describe the development of reasoning in students as

---

*All names in this account are fictitious to ensure the privacy of the participating teachers and school. Their words in quotations are excerpts from transcribed interviews or fieldnotes.

a perennial teaching difficulty rather than a teaching problem. Here they use Barzun's (1981) distinction between "difficulties" and "problems" when considering their teaching work. "Problems are solved or disappear with the revolving times. Difficulties remain" (p. xix). The difficult work of teaching well is an issue that continues to challenge and invigorate those who are thoughtful about their work. "It will always be difficult," Barzun wrote, "to teach well, to learn accurately; to read, write, and count readily and competently; to acquire a sense of history and develop a taste for literature and the arts—in short, to instruct and start one's education or another's" (p. xx).

Moreover, what recent national debate has made increasingly clear is that an understanding of how critical thinking can be taught requires an understanding of the cognitive work of individual teachers. Recent research on effective teaching and national policy recommendations ignore this focus (see Denham and Lieberman, 1980; Gage, 1978; Karweit, 1983; National Commission, 1983; Peterson and Walberg, 1979; Rosenshine, 1983; Shavelson and Dempsey-Atwood, 1976; Shavelson and Stern, 1981; Stallings, 1980). Either they have developed composite descriptions of effective teaching and ignored the unique configuration of skills in individual teachers; or they have overlooked the important role of pedagogical content knowledge in planning curriculum; or they have studied fundamentals and have not attended to higher order thinking skills; or they are based upon outcome measures and have neglected classroom process data; or they have disregarded the structural characteristics of reasoning tasks that profoundly affect classroom order and achievement. Concern about these oversights has shaped this study of secondary teaching.

A study of teaching critical thinking at the secondary level deserves our attention for three reasons. First, it highlights the complexities of teaching and calls to the forefront an understanding of teacher knowledge as well as performance. To teach students to use higher order thinking processes—those processes that require the manipulation of information rather than the reproduction of knowledge—requires more than the refinement of discrete, generic teaching skills. Students must think *about* something. Teaching critical thinking is, therefore, based upon a teacher's broad and deep understanding of subject matter and a representation of that understanding in multiple forms as work activities for students. Thus, critical thinking is context-bound. Its effective strategies vary by subject matter, by an individual teacher's conception of that subject matter, by the way that conception is represented in work tasks for students, and by a teacher's ability to engage and sustain student attention in those tasks. Further, by combining information about academic work that students and teachers are trying to accomplish and their organizational demands, this study highlights the fundamental tension between organizational and instructional processes in classrooms. It calls attention to the significance of this tension for both order and achievement.

A study of the role of teachers' pedagogical content knowledge and classroom order in teaching critical thinking deserves our attention for a second reason. Increased knowledge about the transformation of subject matter understanding into work tasks will increase our effectiveness in pre-service and in-service teacher education. Few case histories of this process exist, and case studies may be our best avenue to understanding this important but little understood process. In addition, a cognitive model of classroom management supplies a better standard for designing programs to enhance the management skills of novice and experienced teachers.

A study of teaching critical thinking deserves attention for a third reason, the centrality of schooling. The secondary school is currently the only social institution specifically designed to develop these cognitive skills in adolescents. If higher order thinking is not promoted in the course of learning to read, compose, and calculate, a student may never have an opportunity to move beyond the literal interpretation of information. No other social organization—not the peer group, the family, religion, or the work site—requires analytical thought in any sort of systematic manner. Thus, if reasoning is not expected as a part of secondary classroom activities, it may never be developed.

This crucial role for secondary teaching is a dominant theme in curriculum today. Both popular and critical literatures have acknowledged the schools' low expectations for higher order processing skills in high school students (see Applebee, 1981, 1984; Boyer, 1983; Clifford, 1984; Forbes and Brown, 1981; Goodlad, 1983; Haney, 1984; Sizer, 1984). This literature has also proposed a variety of school reform measures to increase these skills in students (see Boyer, 1983; Confrey, 1982; Cuban; 1984; de Bono, 1983; Mayer, 1975; Noddings, 1984) or ways to improve the preparation of teachers (see Commons, 1985; Carnegie Task Force, 1986; Lanier, 1986; Smith, 1983). None, however, has based its recommendations upon careful analysis of teachers' knowledge bases for teaching or upon the differences that structural requirements of reasoning tasks place upon teachers and students.

Nonetheless, in order to improve academic instruction effectively, efforts must be founded upon an understanding of how teachers think about content and how they make that understanding explicit for students (Calfee, 1986; Shulman, 1986b). This study extends this line of research. Here, an understanding of teacher knowledge is drawn from teachers' definitions rather than from research. My chief purpose has been to study teacher conceptions of their work and from that to construct a descriptive hierarchy of teacher knowledge. In this study the conception of the process of teaching reasoning is that of a process highly complex, experiential, purposeful, sometimes digressive, and context-bound. Teachers' effectiveness in teaching critical thinking is based on teachers' understanding of their work; hence, it is viewed as tentative, transient, and subject to change rather than fixed, objective, and unchanging.

The concept of teaching reasoning as an exploration of teacher knowledge embodies this experiential view. In experiential analysis (Reinharz, 1984), the role of the researcher is to approach a research setting through the participants' understanding of that world. To impose a perspective from the outside denigrates the worth of that world. The essential task of the experiential is to understand how the researcher's own experience, in that setting along with other data, contributes to an understanding of that culture. Experiential analysis differs from other social science methods only in this data-gathering and -analyzing phase of research; thereafter, as in other methods, the analysis is compared to other bodies of literature in order to establish its relation to the shared community of scholarship. It places a high priority upon detailed, long-term observation and participation in order to conceptualize "interrelationships among classroom variables and the connections between such variables and student achievement" (Doyle, 1977, p. 183). Jackson (1968) and Cusick (1973), for example, who have analyzed the interactive processes of elementary and secondary classrooms, can be seen to assume an experiential view in their conception of the forces, both curricular and interpersonal, that shape students' experiences.

These considerations gave rise to the use of interpretive methods for this study of secondary teaching. In part, justification of the methodology comes from the experiential relationship that connects teacher and researcher. As a researcher, I could not enter a classroom as a neutral observer and expect to understand the highly complex network of relations that a teacher designs and manages. Instead, I entered each classroom as a person with equal interest in the process of teaching reasoning; my knowledge of teaching interacted with that of the participants'. Because I could be explicit about my assumptions, my relationship with participating teachers was honest and was based on mutual respect. Neither researcher nor teachers were unchanged by the relationship. The meaning of the experience, which emerges from open-ended interviews, from offering interpretations, and from talking together, is a shared construction.

Experiential relationships with seven teachers, among them the four who serve as illustrative examples in this study, were established over three months of participation observation and interviews. Bob, Langdon, Linda, and Conrad became interested in participating in the study when approached by their principal, Joseph Grimaldi, who nominated each as an exceptional teacher who challenged students' thinking. These four were selected from the larger group because of the dominance of critical thinking in their teaching, for the richness of the data available on each, and for their illustrative value in understanding teacher knowledge.

Participant observation methodology was used in all four classrooms. I observed in Bob's and Linda's classrooms for five hours per week for two weeks in April 1984, and in Conrad's and Langdon's classrooms for eight hours per week for two weeks in May 1984. In each classroom I took an active role as a shy student. I read the text, listened during discussions, watched demonstrations, and read course descriptions, classroom handouts, assignments, and information recorded on chalkboards and bulletin boards. During all classroom visits I took notes; three class sessions of each teacher, typically on the final three days of observation, were also tape recorded. After leaving school, usually the same day, events were reconstructed into field notes (Erickson, 1972; Smith and Geoffrey, 1968). The principal topics on which notes were made were activities for accomplishing their goals, their presentation of subject matter understanding in explanation and narration, their work tasks for students, and their methods for motivating and sustaining student performance. In addition, I recorded questions about the meaning of these events for further observation. My notes attempted to give a complete account, recording as much detail as could be remembered.

One open-ended interview was held with each teacher prior to observation: in April 1984 with Bob and Linda, and in May 1984 with Conrad and Langdon. These focused upon their goals for students, their understanding of subject matter, their principal activities directed toward accomplishing these goals, their concerns in working with this group of students, and their recent professional development activities. These interviews were tape recorded and later transcribed. In addition, I held two open-ended interviews with Joseph Grimaldi, their principal, in April and May 1984. These focused upon school organization, student population, district and school-sponsored staff development, and community support. Less formal discussions were held with seven of their teacher colleagues. These focused upon school and departmental goals and school climate. I also attended a faculty meeting and a Parent-Teacher-Student Association meeting. Dictaphone notes were made of these interviews and meetings and were later transcribed.

These teaching documents—field note and interview data—were originally coded into content units, coded by brief descriptive phrases related to each teacher's goals and subject matter understanding for teaching. Preliminary interpretations and comments were written as I analyzed field note and interview data. After initial analysis, the data, which now included raw data, descriptive phrases, and theoretical memos (Glaser and Strauss, 1967), were reread in order to identify practices that seemed an embodiment and enactment of the four teachers' pedagogical content knowledge.

Preliminary narrative accounts were also prepared on each teacher. These accounts took the form of an educational criticism (Eisner, 1985), a description and analysis of four classroom experiences, one for each teacher, a session typically occurring toward the end of the observation period as representative of the major conventions of that classroom. Events that preceded or followed each experience were included to illustrate recurring and unique features. These accounts advanced notions of structure of curriculum content and the ways that structure is translated into work tasks for students; they also offered interpretations of classroom management in relation to these goals. The analysis that follows begins with these narrative accounts but also draws from all data gathered on each teacher.

In short, the process of case generation advanced from the individual to the general: "(1) identifying key events or experiences for each informant; (2) interpreting the meaning of the identified instances; (3) identifying themes that related key instances in each case; and (4) identifying a structure that related one case with another" (Wilson and Gudmundsdottir, 1986, p. 4).

These case studies are useful to the recursive nature of theory generation in several ways. Cases show us how teachers enact content in classrooms. As such, they reveal the complexity of teaching, both its classroom interactions and the cognitive activities that form the knowledge base for teaching. Cases thus provide a catalyst in generating a framework and in elaborating upon that framework. Further, case studies can point to dimensions absent in existing frameworks and test emerging theories' applicability to the wisdom of practice.

This analysis of cognition and teaching proceeds thematically. The first two chapters introduce Bob, Langdon, Linda, and Conrad and relate this study to recent scholarship on instruction. Chapter 1, "Four Teachers of Critical Thinking," provides brief portraits of each of the four teachers and introduces the major analytical themes. These exemplars vividly represent characteristics found in all of their observed teaching. Chapter 2, "Cognition in Teaching," presents what is known of the nature of critical thinking, about the knowledge base for teaching, and about organizing and managing classroom activities that promote critical thinking.

The next three chapters focus upon themes in teaching critical thinking that are identified in the portraits and data. Chapter 3, "Teacher Knowledge for Teaching Critical Thinking," analyzes the pedagogical content knowledge, knowledge of students, and of self for the four teachers, including the organizing imagery that shapes both instruction and classroom management. Chapter 4, "Transforming Content into Critical Thinking Tasks," identifies how each teacher represents that content in narration and explanation and how content is understood by students through academic tasks. Chapter 5, "Managing Critical Thinking Tasks," assesses the ways the four teachers provide a supportive environment for intellectual risk-taking through gathering and sustaining student attention to these tasks; it also compares their strategies.

Finally, Chapter 6, "Teaching Critical Thinking as a Cognitive Act," summarizes the major findings from this analysis through a model of teacher knowledge for teaching critical thinking; it discusses implications for schools as organizations and for the professional education of teachers.

The guiding concept for this study is this: The process of teaching reasoning is a complex network of relations among a teacher's knowledge base, instructional decisions, and classroom management and organization, which can be, to varying degrees, articulated by individual teachers. It is a network that, at one level, relates teacher thinking to practice and, at another level, suggests links between participant observation data about individual teachers with ideas about teachers in general. I came to understand the work of Bob, Langdon, Linda, and Conrad as embodying these webs of significance. Although I speak of four individuals, an understanding of how they conceive subject matter content and transform that conception into instructional activities and managerial strategies in the process of teaching sheds light upon secondary teaching more generally.

A final word of caution is in order, however. In this study of teaching critical thinking I have focused solely upon the individual work of four teachers. I have not considered how these teachers were educated or how the school environment supports and sustains their work. These contextual factors are unquestionably influential in promoting reasoning but are beyond the scope of this study. I have also not considered questions of what the standards of teacher performance in this area ought to be. Such policy issues are vitally important, but they are inappropriately formulated from studies of only a few teachers. My purpose is a fundamental first step toward these larger policy issues: to add to the knowledge base of researchers, teacher educators, and teachers about the role of subject matter and pedagogy in teaching critical thinking.

1

Four Teachers of Critical Thinking

BOB POST, HISTORIAN

Bob Post, as chair of the Social Science Department at Castile High School, is the most active of these four teachers in school governance and curriculum development. He is a member of the School Leadership Council, which meets monthly with the principal to coordinate curriculum and to promote professional development. This Leadership Council approves curriculum changes in departmental offerings and reviews individually submitted proposals for curriculum development. As department chair, Bob also participates in the evaluation of the ten tenured and untenured teachers within his department. He is a member of the District Social Science Subject Area Council, a district-wide committee of department heads from each of the eight high schools. The primary focus of the Subject Area Council is curriculum development and other matters directly related to the educational program of students. It reviews, studies, and makes recommendations on all district curricular proposals in social science.

For eighteen months, Bob has been chair of the Computer Literacy Committee at Castile. In that time, this faculty committee has developed and implemented a computer literacy program for both students and faculty. Committee members have developed a four and a half week module that is included in the ninth grade social studies curriculum. They have identified the hardware and software necessary for this program and now monitor the curriculum and the scheduling of the Computer Center. The Committee also offers two-hour workshops for teachers, taught by members of the Committee, on word processing, gradebook data, and programming. Much of Bob's unscheduled time at school is spent supervising this program of working with teachers.

At the departmental level, Bob has provided leadership in curriculum revision. He has worked with other members of his department to incorporate the computer literacy component into all first-year social science courses. He has coordinated a writing component in the freshman program with members of the freshman English staff. He has directed the development of a highly unusual three-year honors program. The recent decision to expand the study of American history to three semesters—the second semester of the sophomore year covers the founding to 1828—was a decision to move through the content more slowly and thoroughly. Previously, preparation for the Advanced Placement exam had absorbed all the available time; the change allows a slower pace and the opportunity to "do a few things better" for more powerful learning.

Both through his own participation and by encouraging his colleagues' participation, Bob actively supports the instructional improvement program. One summer he participated in a ten-week workshop for the National Writing Project; then, with four colleagues, he was instrumental in developing the Castile Writing Project for the English and Social Science Departments. During a summer workshop the following summer, selected members from these two departments developed the instructional packets for eight writing assignments to be taught jointly in ninth grade English and social science classes. Bob volunteered as an early participant in a one-week district-supported program for instructional improvement and clinical supervision. The workshop, based on the work of Madeline Hunter, reviewed lesson planning, learning theory, and classroom management. Bob found its content to be a helpful review of instructional principles, but it was unable to speak to his concerns about sequencing ideas to help students develop thinking skills. He regrets the little available time for teachers to observe clinical teaching skills in others' classrooms; he continues to argue that improved teaching requires time for teachers to build colleagueship and to work together on common problems of teaching. He has encouraged Castile's participation in a federally supported consortium consisting of a county office, a state university, a professional organization, and four public and private schools to improve staff morale and increase participatory decision making in quality circles.

Bob consciously tries to apply this learning to the classroom. For example, he frequently tries to use the early minutes of the class hour for instruction, a suggestion from the clinical teaching workshop, but finds this sometimes results in his forgetting to take roll altogether. His classroom tasks have been substantially influenced by his participation in the writing workshops. His use of graphics, of prewriting activities for generating ideas, and of imaginative written assignments shows the application of his learning in these sessions.

Off-campus, Bob has taken a leadership role in a variety of professional activities. He made a presentation on the quality circles program at a university-sponsored conference. With a colleague from Castile, he presented a teaching workshop on the U.S. Senate at a Hearst Foundation-sponsored conference. He was a university Coe Fellow in U.S. History one summer and spent a second summer at the same university in a computer learning workshop. He is a past member and past president of the Santa Teresa City School District Board of Trustees and a member of the Early Childhood Education Committee of the National Council for the Social Studies. Finally, during the period of this study, he and Langdon attended a two-day workshop, sponsored by the National Endowment for the Humanities, on the bicentennial of the Constitution. Bob's ability to participate in this wide range of professional activity may be influenced, to some extent, by the stability of his teaching assignment: He is the only one of the four who has not changed school assignments or major teaching assignments in the past five years.

Portrait of a History Teacher

Bob is an energetic, slightly balding, slightly disorganized, unassuming, and thoughtful historian. An experienced teacher, he exudes the confidence and openness that his customary dress—an open-necked, button-down shirt, a brown corduroy jacket, and tan pants conveys. One Wednesday morning in April he was leaning on his podium, a transformed audiovisual cart on wheels that held his notes and materials and followed his wanderings, at the front of Room F5 as his first-period honors history class entered. Stepping into the classroom, students automatically checked the roster on the back wall, where scores from last Monday's quiz had been posted. A bright, eager group of thirty-eight, they entered with energy, found their seats, and chattered easily with friends, their voices ricocheting off bare classroom surfaces. They filled all but two of the forty student desks crowded into this small room.

Bob took roll silently this morning, noted Beth's absence on the appropriate slip, and returned papers to Amy and Carin. He closed the door, circled the left side of the room, and rolled his podium to a more central location.

"Ok," he began. "Can I have your attention now, please?" Thirty-eight students hurried to finish their conversation. Mr. Post picked up a dittoed page containing the essay questions for the current unit on "America Secedes from the Empire" and held it up for reference. "Today, I'm going to proceed a little differently than I have for a while." This was today's experimental approach to discussion, the reason for Bob's unusual hesitancy. Charles leaned forward to talk with Brian, in the seat in front of him. Mr. Post frowned toward their corner of the room and the conversation ceased. He leaned on his elbows over the rolling podium, glanced for a moment out the window.

"Today," he continued, "I want you to forget about me as a teacher, although I will retain certain things. Like I'll look at somebody who's working on geometry, Christopher." Mr. Post straightened and peered at Christopher in the last seat of the second row; Christopher closed his book. "Now, today, I'm going to play the role of a substitute teacher. So I want you to think about me as Mr. _____ anybody want to give me a name?"

"Jones," came one reply.

"Yeh, Jones."

"That's good. Jones."

"What about Jellyblob?" Joseph suggested from the back.

Mr. Post wrote "Jellyblob" on the board, then began pacing at the front of the room. His students giggled at his chosen pseudonym. "But," he emphasized by a direct stare at Joseph, "I will still retain my perogatives. Essentially, today I am a substitute. And let me tell you my problem." Bob began pacing again, stopping at the left corner to glance at the view from the window. "My problem was I came to school early but Mr. Post was late; and when I finally got my instructions, they said to go over two essay questions that students are going to write on Friday. Before class, as I was coming in, I pulled out my copy of the questions and read them over." Tom shifted in his desk and it scraped the floor. "It said something about the boys telling me what it is all about. But I frankly don't understand . . . Mr. Post said that probably the girls will do a lot better job than the boys at explaining their essays."

"No way!" Joseph burst out.

"I don't know. Mr. Post may have been wrong. But the question is— and let's focus on that," Mr. Post-Jellyblob read from the dittoed page that was still in his hand, " 'man is basically motivated by his economic self-interest.' John, would you help get us started here? I frankly don't understand what that quote means."

John's answer was mumbled and drowned in his classmates comments.

"Ok, I had the wrong impression." Bob moved halfway down the first aisle on the left before continuing. "It's the young ladies who are going to help me." He repeated the question again, then called on Vicki.

Hands in his pockets and staring at the floor as he listened thoughtfully, Bob walked back to his podium as Vicki also struggled to explain economic self-interest. "Well, economics is what . . . started with the colonies. They all tried for a little economic respect, and when they couldn't do it, they set up these restrictions and took them through the society to all levels."

"You know," Mr. Post-Jellyblob looked up from his listening and, bending forward, commented, "I thought the question was gobbledygook. But I'm not sure that that's not gobbledygook, too." He wrote "economic self-interest" in large block letters on the chalkboard. "I imagine Mr. Post doesn't print as well as that, does he?" There was a chorus of responses to this personal aside. The quality of Mr. Post's chalkboard writing and art-work was a subject of much discussion. Nonetheless, his graphic represen-tations of concepts and their relationships are a salient feature of this classroom experience.

"Is this simply saying," he pointed to the words, "that people, that all of us—you and me and everybody else—are basically after the big bucks? Elizabeth?"

"Yes. I think that when it comes down to people doing anything it is because they're angry because they're losing money or because they're being stopped from making more money. People are motivated by that and just want more money."

Mr. Post-Jellyblob continued to direct the discussion from an exploration of the motivations for political conflict toward an application of these prin-ciples to the events in American colonial history from 1600 to 1770. He asked Ruth to speak louder so David could hear her comment about the Stamp Act.

"I *said* that England was taking money from the colonies without the colonies' consent. Ok? Thus, the colonies felt that it was wrong, and so instead of paying England, they boycotted and started the revolution."

"Ok," Mr. Post-Jellyblob continued. "So the change—if I understand what Ruth was saying—the change, the movement in history, comes from the boycott. The boycott was really what was happening, and if one wants to understand that boycott, what one does is look to the fact that the colonies are getting pinched economically. They're concerned about having to dish out the money for stamps. Susan?"

"It wasn't really against the colonies that the Stamp Act was looking. The Stamp Act came about because England had got itself into . . . was worried about being able to take care of its debts. So I think it was more the English that were causing the conflict because the colonists were just protecting what was rightfully theirs. It was a matter of principle."

Greg, however, was not as convinced as the others that the Stamp Act was motivated purely by economic considerations. He asked for clarification on the political changes. In replying to this request, Bob called his students' attention to an earlier reading in the unit. "Jensen," he began, referring to the author of their reading, "Jensen seemed to be saying that there was quite a movement for people to gain political power in the colonies. I thought he said something about the Stamp Act being used to gain political power. Susan?"

"Yes, the colonists were using the fact that they were being taxed without representation as . . . the principle was wrong then so they were using it as a basis to rebel. It wasn't really economic, but it was more the principle of the matter that they were being taxed without representation. And it meant that they were trying to gain more than lower taxes; it was their means of rebellion so they could gain more advantage and political power."

"Ok, so you feel, then, if you were writing your paper, at least one part of your paper would argue that the colonists were concerned with political issues. That was really what was motivating them, and that they were sort of covering up, maybe, some economic questions."

Susan continued. "They were economically motivated, but we were motivated by principles."

"Interesting thesis," Mr. Post-Jellyblob noted. "Do you understand what Susan is saying? She's suggesting that maybe change comes from economic motivation in England coming into conflict with political motivation in the colonies." He wrote these terms and their sources on the board. "Now, Mr. Post says that I'm supposed to divide the time equally between these two questions—do I still have half an hour left here?"

You have four minutes," several reminded him.

"Four minutes!" His students giggled at Mr. Post-Jellyblob's consternation. "Ok, let's see how helpful the men can be, very quickly." He read the second essay question, a comparison of readings by Jensen and Rossiter on the Declaration of Independence. "Tell me, Anthony, how did Rossiter look at the Declaration?"

"Umm, I guess he was against it," Tony mumbled.

"He was against the Declaration of Independence? He was not, my good man. John?"

"Well, it was an agreement between all the people, he would have said, that made the Declaration of Independence. So everybody had consensus. Some people went halfway and other people went halfway and they agreed on the middle road."

"So the Declaration, you feel in Rossiter's view, represents the consensus viewpoint of all the colonies? Good. Mr. Post left some kind of note saying that the Declaration of Independence represented a consensus of American opinion and was a document that symbolized, then, some Americans coming together. Denis, tell me, how does Jensen view that Declaration?"

Denis sat lost in thought.

"Mr. Post was right. The boys must have slept last night." Just then the bell rang, indicating the end of Period 1. Mr. Post, back in his own role, interrupted its buzzing. "Rossiter and Jensen seem a little weak in this discussion. Now, the Declaration of Independence represents something very clear to Jensen. You ought to be able to recognize that. Please take a look at that issue and check your understanding of it. If you don't understand more than we discussed today, you will not be able to write your essay on Friday. Ok, have a good day."

Mr. Post's students picked up their books and spilled into the corridor outside.

The fundamental concept organizing Bob's teaching is the concept of power. History records the passage of power from one group to the next; in this discussion, students were to identify those human or psychological forces that motivated British and colonial actions in that period shortly before the Revolution. Earlier discussion had focused upon motivations of the representatives at the First Continental Congress. This concept is further played out in the imagery of the game. Bob instigates male-female rivalry by suggesting that "probably the girls will do a lot better job than the boys at explaining their essays" and "Mr. Post was right; the boys must have slept last night." He also sets up a game through the persona of "Mr. Jellyblob." By assuming the role of a substitute, Bob can pose as an uninformed adult who asks naive questions. This permits him to probe student answers further than usual. But the role also sets up the student game of "get the substitute" and inspires outbursts and actions. Within this conception and its instructional representations, his students come to understand the meaning of history.

LANGDON SELHORST, POLITICAL SCIENTIST

As a member of Bob's department, Langdon Selhorst is active in curriculum development activities and works toward establishing a norm of shared responsibility. As chair of the departmental subcommittee to reorganize the government curriculum, he had included this norm in a collective discussion of choice for a draft of the department course outline for government.

Unit 6 can consist of one or more units at the instructor's pleasure, but unit outlines are to be presented to the department for discussion and reaction; it is understood that what a teacher decides in curriculum and instruction is to a large extent a matter of academic freedom, but we believe that continuing dialogue about evolving units of instruction is beneficial both to an individual's growth as a teacher and to congruency and achievement of departmental goals.

In addition, he has successfully argued to include in this draft one of his own teaching goals: "to instill a joy of learning even at the risk of spending hours of hard work at it." He serves as Castile's representative on a district committee to develop competencies in government.

In more informal ways, Langdon builds both interdepartmental and intradepartmental colleagueship. At his suggestion, he and Bob attended a two-day National Endowment for the Humanities workshop on the Constitution; he wrote the application, garnered administrative support, applied for travel funds, and proposed a way to bring the Constitutional Bicentennial to Castile. Because he and Linda share the same conference period and regularly work at their desks in the English-Social Science Office, they speak frequently about the shortcomings of the model of teaching promoted by the Clinical Teaching Workshops and its alternatives. On one occasion, Langdon shared an article from an educational journal that he found thought-provoking (Dawes, 1984). Ideas on how to maintain the art in teaching in a technically oriented community animated their conversation for several days. Like the other three teachers, he has participated in the clinical teaching workshop and computer learning workshops for teachers.

Langdon transferred to Castile three years ago and began teaching government for the first time in his career. Although he had not formally studied political science since his undergraduate program, this time he began by analyzing his own learning patterns and applying them to the curriculum. His most recent learning experience has been at the computer, which he has adapted to his work both as a teacher and as a lawyer. This experience has confirmed for him the importance of active involvement in learning; he mastered the computer by working with it rather than by reading the manuals. In this classroom, this principle underlies the weekly writing tasks that are designed for students to explore ideas by actively manipulating them into a coherent statement. In a forthcoming sabbatical he will pursue graduate study in political science to further these understandings.

Portrait of a Government Teacher

Langdon is a dark, imposing man, full of energy and life. He strode assertively into Room F8, taking full advantage of his six-foot frame. Dressed like the lawyer he is, he exudes a passion for teaching and learning and a passion for history and the governmental process.

Immediately, six students circled Langdon's podium to figure their grades, clear absences, and discuss missing assignments. It was a Thursday in May, only four weeks before these seniors graduate. Langdon engaged them in amused conversation while emptying his briefcase, arranging his materials, and hanging up his jacket. The rest of the class entered and picked up conversation in clumps throughout the classroom, the sound of their voices reverberating in the sparsely decorated room. At the bell, Langdon took roll, noting eight absences.

"Ok," he began. Student conversation stopped. "Since the jeopardy letters went home, I've had a chance to get to know some of your parents better, and they're nice people. I always like to talk to your parents, because every once in a while they ask how their son or daughter can improve their grade. And I have some suggestions, so if any of you'd like me to call your parents, I'll know you're going to use my opinion about improvement.

"Now I have discovered that I'm going to have to postpone the test until Monday. I know that causes you a great deal of pain, but I will still be here today for the help session." He then teased David and Sergio about wearing caps in the classroom. His combination of teasing and serious information was read carefully by these students; they understood the postponement of the test but giggled at the teasing, knowing that only a few would receive failure notices.

The opening ritual completed, Langdon moved to an academic focus for the remainder of the hour. He began by explaining his evaluation plan for the essay exam, now postponed until Monday. Pointing to a mimeographed unit outline, he added: "Here you have the test questions; you have all these outlines and now you've got my answer sheet. So it should be nothing but straight A's—and I look forward to reading your papers.

"Today I want to take us further down the pike and I want to finish the electoral college and the difference between the two parties. First, let me just make sure that you have no questions about the nomination process or about the election process that we reviewed yesterday. Does anybody have any questions about the nomination process?"

Ted admitted to a nebulous notion about balloting at the nominating convention. Langdon returned to yesterday's concept, the presidenial nomination process, and reviewed the chronology of that process, from its formal beginning with the first set of primaries in New England to the convention in August. "That's the process. But the battle is to win what through the primaries and caucuses? What is the battle? The goal?" Having satisfied Ted, Langdon reviewed the three purposes of the convention: the platform, the candidates, and the coalition. Mark asked if Mondale's failure to enter the forthcoming convention without locking up the nomination would hurt the party.

"In fact, a lot of people say that could be the worst thing that can happen to the Democrats. I am not at all convinced of that. In fact, if you look at the history of these conventions, there was a time when American politics were shaped by the open conventions and the deals that were made in smoke-filled rooms. The Democrats might be just one hellavalot better off having to deal with the political reality of the divisions in the old coalitions. At this point, if Mondale goes in with a 55 percent or 54 percent control of the delegates, that could lead to greater division. In any case, let's get past the nomination process and get back to the election process, unless you have any further questions." Langdon was back on track; the first 25 minutes of Period 3 were gone. There were no further questions.

"Ok. Now the nominees emerge from their conventions. Now, the question is this . . ." Langdon stopped to add to his board notes. "On election day, when you go to the polls and you pull the handle for Reagan or Mondale, what are you really doing? Who are you really voting for?"

"Electors," came a chorus of replies.

"Electors. Don't get the delegates, who are the people who go to the nominating convention, confused with the electors, who vote for president." Langdon continued this presentation, reviewing the number of electors per state, the election of electors, and the electoral vote.

"Has a president ever won," David asked, "who has had fewer total votes?"

"Yes, in the election of 1824 and 1876." Langdon briefly reviewed the popular election of Andrew Jackson in 1824 and the 1876 contest between Tildon and Hayes. "So the electoral college has not always chosen the people's choice. But what was the electoral college designed to do?"

"To control the masses." Ted spoke up.

"Yes, it was to safeguard the power of the masses. And the hope of the founding fathers was that, at a crucial point in history when the country is badly divided, instead of a man being chosen by a mob, who could be a man of a white horse and a great tyrant along the lines of Caesar or Napoleon, the electors could have the courage to stand against the mob and pick somebody else. And guess what? All of the great disputed elections in American history—the elections of 1800, 1824, 1860, and 1876, in all of which the electoral college had crises—every one of those was in the midst of a great national political crossroad. Each of those marks a transfer of power from one bloc to another, at least a struggle for it. So the electoral college was at the heart of some of the greatest crises in American history.

"Now the question is, why do we have a two-party system?"

"So if neither party achieves a majority, then neither has a popular president. It's a safeguard." Ted was still following.

"No, that's not quite right. You're close, but that doesn't answer the question. Why do we have a two-party system? Mr. Lacrois?"

Mark began. "Isn't it so that the smaller party can anticipate the faults of the major party and form a coalition."

"Wait a minute. You're not answering my question. You're anticipating the question. Why do we have a two-party system?"

"So we can have a majority vote."

"Because you can win the presidency easily, if what?"

"There are only two parties."

"There are only two parties. If there are only two parties that get electoral votes, then they will decide the presidency. And therefore, there is tremendous incentive on both parties to do what?"

"To please more people." Lyn entered the conversation.

"To please more people and when a third party starts to get popular enough to be able to get electoral votes, they will tend to form allies and co-opt it and bring it into one or the other side. Does that make sense?" Langdon had now spent 40 minutes reviewing and reteaching the nomination and election processes.

With one final summary of the three steps in the election process, he compared it to a parlimentary system. "At heart and root, our system is a parlimentary democracy. If it were not for the electoral college, we would have a system very much like other parlimentary models. So those are the three points that you need to remember in this area for the test." Langdon was now ready to move on to new material.

"And, now, my question is, what is the difference between the Democrats and the Republicans?" Langdon then summarized the historical coalition of factions in the Republican and Democratic parties and the ways those coalitions are currently in transition. "If we cast the question somewhat differently and ask which party has the more liberal and which party has the more conservative factions, the Democratic factions will tend to lean somewhat to the left and the Republican factions somewhat to the right, under those circumstances." To illustrate the relationship, Mr. Selhorst shaped his hands into an overlapping fan. "But that is not because, primarily, of ideology. It is because of the nature of the interest groups represented in the factions that make up the coalition."

With an eye on the clock, Langdon summarized the hour. "Now, I'm going to hold my help session today. Tomorrow, I will show you what had happened in the history of the United States to transform the American party system from ideological parties to popular parties. Your test will be on Monday and I will just send progress reports to those people who need help and enhancement in their social lives."

Langdon finished his last line just as a buzzer sounded. Students picked up their books and filed toward the door. Only Laura turned back to look for a lost book.

A major goal for this government course is an understanding of the concepts necessary for an informed citizenry. Langdon includes in this list of concepts an understanding of the political process, particularly the nomination and election processes discussed in this classroom experience. Further, his emphasis on the actual difference between the two political parties works toward his goal of developing independent thought; he wishes students to understand that the differences between Republicans and Democrats come from traditional coalitions of factions rather than ideology. Inherent in each of these is the image of "the great debate" or "battle for men's minds," a powerful metaphor that organizes Langdon's teaching and helps to convey his image of political realities.

LINDA REED, LITERARY ANALYST

As the newest of the four teachers to Castile, Linda Reed is especially aware of the school's "wonderfully exciting and exhausting" atmosphere. This feeling she attributes to Joseph Grimaldi's leadership as principal and to her teaching colleagues. She regularly confers with other English teachers during her conference period. She speaks with Dr. Hoffman, the coordinator of the English honors program, about her analyses of sophomore and junior honors students' learning needs and about locating texts for her revised Senior Seminar. With her department chair, she discusses scheduling options for the coming fall. She appreciates her colleagues' trust in her ability to revitalize the senior honors program. She also confers with Langdon. The comfortable disorder of her desk in the English-Social Science Department area invites this collaboration.

Along with the other teachers in this study, Linda has participated in a number of professional activities. She, too, was an early participant in the ten-week National Writing Project summer workshop and in the one-week clinical teaching workshop, which she found a useful reminder of her professional education. She has participated in summer workshops at a local university and in three professional oganizations: National Council of Teachers of English, State Association of Teachers of English, and Regional Council of Teachers of English. She has completed a career increment proposal, a program of professional development and self-study, which provides salary increases for those teachers at the top of the salary schedule. At Castile, she has participated in three computer workshops for teachers—word processing, data base management, and computer-assisted instruction—and has purchased her own microcomputer to support her professional work.

Portrait of an English Teacher

On a Friday in April, the last school day before spring vacation, Linda entered Room E7 several minutes before the beginning of Period 3, her arms loaded with copies of *The Bear*. She headed toward the table centered at the front of the room to set down her load. That accomplished, she filed her purse in the desk, set her new glasses on top, and began to speak with individual students about the *King Lear* papers due that day. Her seventeen Senior Seminar students—seven others were absent—streamed in. Talking continued in animated fashion past the bell.

"Ok," Ms. Reed concluded her individual discussion and interrupted all talkers, "let's begin." She leaned against the table at the front, considering her decision to use this last hour before vacation as a transitional period completing the study of Lear and introducing Faulkner. "First, today, look around the room and see all the cowards. . . . " The hour began as it usually did, with a humorous reminder about standards and expectations. "Cowards" were those who had not planned their time well and chose absence to mask their unfinished essays. Linda's teaching is characterized by these high expectations, both for developing the intellectual skill of literary analysis and essay organization and for learning the important details of sentence structure and punctuation.

"What I want to know," Rob began, "is do these people have . . . do they have the whole vacation to write their papers?"

"It's a late paper," Ms. Reed was responding directly to Rob's question.

"And it is a grade lower; and they must have been aware of that when they were weighing the consequences of today's absence."

Heather picked up on this comment. "Well, is there any extra penalty for the fact that they have an entire week to do it?"

"I would like to assess them an extra penalty, but . . . you know your classmates better than I do. They are obviously not going to work seven days on this paper. In fact, what will happen is. . . . "

"They won't put in the time." Jayne knew the absentees.

Linda returned to the two tasks for the day, proofreading and introducing a new text. "At least one student in this class can stand up and testify to the fact that the proofreading on the last paper was helpful because one of you was not here and missed its benefits. I'm going to give you about ten minutes. Remember that you're too close to the paper now; you know what it should say. You're not proofreading now for content—it's too late for that." Linda's students giggled in recognition of her truth. "But what you can do is find the careless mistakes, primarily two or three things: punctuation, commas, and check for run-on sentences or comma splices. If you're not sure, raise your hand. Use me. That's what I get paid for."

"Then you do get paid for this?" Heather was quick on the pick-up again.

"I don't get paid much, but I do get paid. Ok. Ten minutes. Who does not have a paper?" The fourteen students with papers traded them and moved their desks to form themselves into random clumps of twos, threes, and fours. Gordon and Patty exchanged papers. Andrea, Trish, Jayne, and Jessica worked together. Paul proofread Nathan's paper while Nathan read his. Marc, Adolpho, and Dave formed another group. Claire and Khalid worked alone. All groups conversed about the papers, Lear, college admissions, and Senior Government Day.

Rob, Janis, and Heather gathered at the back of the room to confer with Ms. Reed about their uncompleted papers. After checking with them, Linda immediately focused on the groupings. She stopped to look over Paul's shoulder and answer questions about appropriate wording. She spoke to Claire and Khalid, while noticing Khalid's uncustomary reluctance to show his work. She encouraged Dave, Marc, and Adolpho to work more seriously on proofreading. She answered editing questions for Andrea, Trish, and Claire. Her students continued in animated discussion over the spelling of "tragedy" and semicolons.

After twenty minutes, she collected most of the essays and set them on her desk, then leaned again against the front table. Holding up *The Bear*, she began the second half of her lesson. "Now this is a great book, and when you finish your proofreading, I want to get you started on *The Bear*. Those of you who are here today are going to have a great advantage. Besides the full grade on your paper, you're going to be miles ahead of your classmates. I'm going to get you started, to give you some help. This is going to be the most difficult reading assignment you've done since you've been in high school." Linda's discussion today was much more directive than her usual introductions to new material.

"Even more difficult than *Portrait of an Artist?*" Nathan asked.

"Worse than *Portrait?*" Janis added.

"Oh, no!" Jayne looked dismayed.

"When you come back from vacation, you will have the first actual reading assignment in this book. However, what will help you most is if you will read the entire *The Bear* over vacation. Faulkner's style is both marvelous and incredibly difficult. It requires, at least, a tremendous reading ability. If you will read the whole thing once, straight through in one sitting, you will be miles ahead."

"Is it the vocabulary that's hard?" Heather interrupted.

"What is difficult is his sentence structure. It's not just the vocabulary. There are sentences that are an entire page long." She pointed out one particularly long one in the text. Then, as she had with other readings, Linda produced a dittoed series of study questions to direct students' reading and led the moaners in a halting review of the story of Abraham and Isaac and Benjamin and Joseph.

"But that's not what concerns me today. What concerns me today is how to read this novella. Now, look at page 111—and it will probably help me if I put my new glasses on, since the print is so small." Linda's new glasses were frequently the subject of self-directed teasing. "I mentioned that it will help to read the entire piece all at once. What will happen as you read is that the sentences will sweep by you. And I mean that literally. You have to get rolling with them. But if you put the book down, if you lose your place or get up to answer the telephone, this is one of those strange books that you can't put down and then immediately pick back up and start right where you stopped. You almost always have to go back a page, two pages, sometimes three pages."

"To where the sentence starts," Gordon added. His classmates giggled.

"That's right. Because you lose the train of thought."

" 'Wait, Mom, let me finish this sentence,' " Heather pantomimed a home conversation.

"That's right. What makes this book so marvelous, of course, is that once you get through it and figure out what it means, it's sort of like climbing Mt. Everest.

"Ok, the opening sentence is very easy." Linda began reading.

There was a man and a dog too this time. Two beasts, counting Old Ben, the bear, and two men, counting Boon Hogganbeck, in whom some of the same blood ran which ran in Sam Fathers, even though Boon's was a plebeian strain of it and only Sam and Old Ben and the mongrel Lion were taintless and incorruptible (Stewart and Bethurum, 1954, p. 111).

While her seventeen students poured over their texts, she read the opening two paragraphs with cadence and meaning. When she finished, her students sighed.

"It does make you wonder about a teacher's thoughts in assigning this!" Patty expressed her classmates' initial reaction to the sentence structure.

"Once you get the feeling for this, it's marvelous. You just have to get into it." Linda continued reading with rhythm and meaning to the bottom of the second page.

"Now, what did I do that you should probably do when you read this book?"

"Read it aloud," was the chorus reply. Then Linda's students giggled at the thought of reading to their parents.

"I'm serious. If you will read this to someone . . . this is a book to read in long phrases and clumps. Try to read the appositives and those prepositional phrases and the participles, and all those grammatical units. You have to get those into some kind of verbal–auditory sense. You can't read this book with your eyes; you have to read it with your ear. And if you are a good ear-reader—by that I mean that you can read with your mouth shut but your ear going, and some of you can—you can read this book without reading it aloud. But if you can't ear-read, then you should read it aloud. And it will fall into place. Those first few pages will be extremely difficult, but you may get so used to the style that you become addicted to it and you'll want to read everything that Faulkner wrote."

Nathan rolled his eyes at this possibility. Others giggled and muttered, "Oh, yeah!"

"I'm serious about this. But you've got to get used to the style to begin with. That's why I suggest you will be a long way ahead of your classmates, who chose to stay home in a cowardly fashion, if you will read the book over vacation. Find a beautiful sunny spot . . . "

Linda's students giggled, again, at the thought of *The Bear* at the beach or in the Palm Springs air.

At that moment, the bell rang. Linda collected book cards and asked to have the *King Lear* books left on the chair by the door. The students who had already turned in an essay filed slowly out of the room. Claire remained to ask one more question about proofreading; Marc poured over his paper one last time before handing it to Ms. Reed and leaving for chemistry.

In this first year of teaching a new course, Linda emphasizes equally process and content. In defining her goals for students, she speaks at length, with great specificity, about the analytical and composing skills necessary to understand literature. She stresses careful reading, as in this introduction to *The Bear*, and close analysis. She expects students to identify tone and voice in literature. Students regularly practice these skills, in discussion of assigned readings, in short weekly advanced placement analyses of new material, and in culminating essays. But because of difficulty in locating appropriate literature, Linda is less definite about the literary canon. Some literary themes are stressed explicitly—for example, the brief review of the biblical stories of Abraham and Isaac. Others, such as psychological motivations in *King Lear*, are an implicit part of discussion. In future years, Linda's image of the journey may emphasize the content of literature—expeditions have destinations as well as procedures—but this year the image equally supports content and process. Reading Faulkner is like climbing Mt. Everest: It is a formidable accomplishment requiring courage and endurance.

CONRAD RIZZO, PHYSICIST

As Science Department chair, Conrad Rizzo's formal collegial relationships are similar to Bob's. Conrad is also a member of the School Leadership Council, a member of the District Science Subject Area Council, and participates in the evaluation of the six tenured and untenured members of his department. He is proud of the rigor in Castile's science program and regularly argues to maintain it. For example, he continues to use the old physics text, published in 1972, rather than a newer district-adopted one because of its emphasis on word problems; he supplements the more recent physical understandings through classroom narration. These high standards are evident in the results of a university-sponsored study of secondary curriculum; compared to seven regional participating high schools, Castile's physics curriculum had the largest enrollment and the greatest selectivity reported. Like Bob, Conrad is a member of the Computer Committee and, as a volunteer, teaches workshops for teachers in gradebook data management and word processing.

Moreover, Conrad's enthusiasm for teaching and for his program is boundless. Like Langdon and Linda, Conrad transferred to Castile from another district high school. Upon his arrival three years ago, he began teaching physics for the first time in his career. Although he had not studied physics since his own training fifteen years before, he approached this new assignment by analyzing his own learning patterns and applied those perceptions to the curriculum. As he has grown in confidence with physical concepts, he seeks their ordinary application. To support this new learning, he has designed a forthcoming sabbatical of university coursework and workshop participation to broaden and deepen this understanding. During the summer he will participate in a workshop at a federal research laboratory and at a science museum; during the academic year he will undertake a full year of graduate work in physics. He participated as an early volunteer in the clinical teaching workshop and in the computer learning workshops for teachers. He has adapted the computer to his classroom needs: Grades are recorded and available for student viewing; departmental equipment inventories are kept; tests are constructed and revised; and students assist in previewing software prior to purchase.

Conrad's hard work and high energy have been richly rewarded. Three times since his arrival at Castile he has been selected by students as Teacher of the Year. He views this honor with pride and embarrassment, acknowledging the high expectations it places on his work. Although he has had opportunities to move to more lucrative positions outside of education, he has chosen to remain at Castile because of the intellectual challenges and opportunities for professional leadership which teaching continues to provide him.

Portrait of a Physics Teacher

Conrad is, in a word, charismatic. Unlike his fellow faculty members, whose dress reflect the more conservative '80s, he is an unconventional young man with a beard, tee shirt, and jeans. He prides himself in his unusual teaching performance and in his relationship with students.

On a Friday afternoon in May, eighteen of the fifth-period physics students eagerly dumped their books at lab stations and clustered in groups for talk. This classroom had a busy, energized atmosphere.

One minute before the starting bell, Mr. Rizzo entered quickly into Room B6 from the storeroom and stepped to the center platform, behind the demonstration table. Recognizing the sign to begin, his students moved toward their stools at the lab stations, but the talking continued. "All right-y," he began. "I would like to review dispersion, which we discussed yesterday." Three stools scraped the floor as students settled into their places.

"Well, before we get started . . . since you're interrupting me, I'll interrupt you." Mr. Rizzo now had his students' full attention. He continued in a low, lyrical voice. "It's my understanding that should any of us ever need a loan, there is somebody in this room who has an additional $2,000 to spare." Seventeen heads grinned toward Randy at the back. Conrad led Randy in a humorous interchange about his recently awarded scholarship before continuing the review of yesterday's lesson: the parts of the electromagnetic spectrum, the formula for calculating wavelengths, and the formula for determining the energy of a wave. He once again illustrated color separation in a prism, then introduced color mixing, today's lesson focus.

"There are an enormous number of frequencies in this arc." He moved his arms in a large fanshape. "How many are there? An infinite number of possible frequencies. But in general, low ones appear to be red to our eyes. High ones appear to be violet and blue to our eyes." He described the physical properties of the Young Helmholtz color vision theory as light frequencies "tickling" particular retinal cones. "When you see something black, none are being tickled." He raised both arms, palms upward, as if to express amazement.

In recognition of this word play on her last name, Laura Black booed. Her classmates slowly caught the pun and giggled.

"Ah," continued Conrad, "the essence of the Happy Donut." Then he resumed the discussion of color vision theory. "In general, you see The Big Three. From The Big Three, all the other colors come. They are called the . . . "

"Primary colors," his students chorused.

"Primary colors."

"I always wondered," Bill asked, "about yellow."

"But that's a primary pigment," Laura added.

"I love it," Conrad continued, moving closer to his students. "I'm glad you said it now. Here we go—we are going to right now avoid a lot of confusion during the period by making it very clear what we're talking about and what we're *not* talking about." He clarified the distinction between pigment and light.

"So it's green light?" Bill reiterated.

"Yes, it's green light mixed with red light that makes yellow light. And I want to make one more point about these Big Three—red, green, blue. You put those *lights* together, you get all the colors." He walked forward to lean one elbow on a lightbox on the center table. "And if you don't believe me, I want you to go home tonight and look at your idiot box. Walk up to your television set tonight, turn the TV off, and get real close to that puppy. You're going to see a lot of dots all over that screen. And you know what color those dots are?"

"Red, blue, and green," came the chorus.

"So you see, Physics-land and TV-land are somehow connected." Students giggled at these shifts from serious concepts to pop culture and back again. Conrad began to insert color filters into the lightbox, showing first a circle of red, then one of blue and green. Where the circles slightly overlapped each other, white appeared. Throughout the following color mixing discussion, Conrad moved quickly between the lightbox, where he demonstrated the additions, and the board, where he recorded the formulas. The room alternated between dark and light. "Let's pop that up here on the board and get that into our notes. R plus B plus G gives us what?" He wrote a formula on the board. "What I propose to do now is to show you what combinations of only two colors will do. So pick a combination."

"Blue and green," Susan suggested.

"Blue and green. Ok. It's your choice." Conrad added more formulas to the list on the board. "Now, we can see the color that we're going to get either by putting blue and green together . . . "

"Or," Randy added, "by subtracting red from white."

"Or by taking red from white." Conrad wrote once more. He returned to the lightbox and the room was again in darkness. Where the blue and green overlapped, cyan [greenish-blue] light flooded the small screen. He added red to produce white light, then subtracted the red to leave cyan again. Then he showed the cyan filter and added red to produce white light. Cyan had been shown in all its combinations.

The lights back on, Conrad similarly demonstrated by formula the combinations producing yellow. Then he bent over to insert something else into the lightbox. "Now, look at that! Oooooooooo! I've got a little stick back here. I thought you might get bored just mixing these, so I thought I'd tickle your heads a little more. This stick—just to show you that it's no trick here—is just a stick." He took it out and, like a magician, exhibited it, then inserted it three times during his next questions. "Now, you can see, if you put the stick in the yellow light and the yellow light doesn't get there, the shadow is black. And, as you can see, if you put the stick in the blue, the shadow turns black. But my question is, how can the shadow be blue there and yellow here? I've never seen a yellow shadow."

John tried a hypothesis. "It blocks the yellow and blue."

"I think what we all might want to do before we . . . ."

"Is to think." Randy knew what was coming.

"Good, I think what we all might want to do is to all think by ourselves for a second and see if we can slug it out. I have a blue shadow and I have a yellow. There's no trick. It's just one stick."

"Mr. Rizzo, the lights are coming from different sources." John began again.

"Ah, there's my boy. Keep going Buckeroo."

"The light's coming from different sources so when the stick is blocking the blue, it allows the yellow to go through where there would be blue."

"Attaboy. There you go."

"And vice versa."

"Sure, and 'versey-vicey.' You see . . . one stick but the lights back there are in different locations. So when the stick blocks out the yellow, the yellow can't combine with the blue; but what does get there is the blue. And blue plus blue is . . . blue. 'Blue on blue'," he warbled. "I thought that might keep your attention, today. Keep tuned in; we're going to do more." He demonstrated the combinations producing magenta and the necessity of having three primaries rather than one primary and one complementary to produce the full range of color.

Charlie predicted one last combination: "If you put cyan and yellow light together, then you'd get green, wouldn't you? Because cyan takes away red and the yellow takes away the blue, but you'd still have green left."

"Charlie's predicting that we'd get a green. Let's do it on the board first and see how it works." Conrad pointed to the complete list of formulas for color combinations. Then, remembering that the lightbox only added colors but could not subtract them, he took the two filters from the box and gave them to Charlie to overlap and hold to the light. "What do you see, Charlie?"

"Green light."

"Green light just like you had predicted. Isn't that a wowser?" Using complementary lights, he demonstrated the stick and shadows again, then explained the ways these light principles are exhibited at the science museum, a field trip scheduled later in the month. He also referred students to the chapter on light in an alternative textbook that he recommended for their weekend reading. "That just about winds up today."

Daniel asked a final question. "Mr. Rizzo, when you combine complementary colors, is it white?"

"When you combine them? When you combine them it's white; when you filter them, it's black." The lesson over, students broke into conversation clusters throughout the room; at the bell, they finished their chatter before filing out. Conrad stopped Chan to talk about fishing before clearing the board and stacking the filters in preparation for sixth period.

For Conrad, the content of physics is composed of three major and fifteen minor concepts held together by a common socialization or set of experiments. This elaboration and the more observable nature of physical concepts permit more focused lessons; the lightbox demonstration, for example, concentrates entirely upon the concepts of mixing and filtering color. Colors are mixed by the application of formulas and by the insertion of filters into the box. The primary thematic image in this presentation is magic. In Conrad's thinking, the existence of physical principles project wonder and fantasy into daily life. "Physics-land" and "TV-land" are magically related because a Sony Trinitron is based on the three primary colors of light. Conrad inserts these attention-getting interruptions, particularly ones directed at students, into his presentations to motivate hard work and maintain student attention.

THE VOICES OF TEACHERS

Although highly individual, Bob Post, Langdon Selhorst, Linda Reed, and Conrad Rizzo each represent history, government, English, and physics teachers familiar to us. One of the reasons for the differences they illustrate is that each draws from a different pedagogical content knowledge, one component of the knowledge base necessary to influence effective learning. Yet beneath their sharp disagreements, there is more than a little consensus about the relationship between critical thinking and hard work, and the relationship between teacher and student. This is because, in spite of their differences, they all share a common educational and moral vocabulary that stresses intellectual challenge, verbal acuity, diligence, and humor.

Bob, Langdon, Linda, and Conrad are seasoned professionals, each with more than fourteen years of teaching experience. In their academic background, they are far more grounded in their subject matter than a typical secondary education major (Kerr, 1983). All have undergraduate majors in a discipline and have completed their professional education as graduate students. Bob is an historian with an undergraduate degree from a small selective university, a Master of Arts in Teaching degree and professional education from an Ivy League university, and further work at a prestigious law school and London University. He has been teaching twenty-three years. After coursework at two Ivy League universities, Langdon completed an undergraduate major in English with a minor in social studies at a large state university in the West. He has a master's degree and teaching certification from the same university and a law degree from an independent law school; in addition to teaching he maintains a small law practice. He has been teaching nineteen years. Linda earned undergraduate and graduate degrees in English from a large state university with a double minor in French and philosophy. Beyond these degrees, she has completed an additional seventy-five credits of university coursework, including certification. She has been teaching eighteen years. Conrad graduated from a prestigious research university with a major in biological sciences and a minor in physical sciences; he fulfilled his teaching certification at a state university and has accomplished an additional forty hours of university coursework. His recent academic development has been limited by his work schedule; he finds it difficult to find time to return to school for additional units when spending more than eighty hours each week on teaching. He has been teaching fifteen years.

All four teachers have achieved a mastery state (Feiman-Nemser, 1983) in their experience, characterized by a sense of confidence and ease and by a concern with student learning and its appropriateness. Although teachers more typically view learning to teach as occurring only during student teaching, these four conceive it as part of the work of a teacher and are continuing to learn. In the last five years, in addition to university-based coursework, all four have participated in district-sponsored faculty development workshops, in discipline-based professional organizations, in individually designed development programs, and in curriculum change programs. Thus, they are solidly grounded in subject matter and accept learning to teach as an on-going aspect of their daily activities. They are active learners themselves and translate that knowledge and experience into their professional and classroom activities.

All four are respected faculty members on one school's staff. In its demographics and program, this school has little to distinguish it from other public suburban high schools. It is a school of 1,561 students, one of seven comprehensive and continuation high schools in a high school district in the West. Because of its attractive programs and reputation for good teaching, the recent decrease in student population has not been as dramatic as at other district schools. A more significant change, however, the result of a district transfer policy, is an increasing ethnic population. In 1984, Castile's minority population was slightly smaller than the district's, 23.89 percent compared to 26.01 percent. Here, minority students are Asian (13.1 percent), Hispanic (8.4 percent), black (2.1 percent), and Native American (0.3 percent).

Moreover, in order to meet the needs of a more varied student population, Castile has diversified its strong academic program for college-bound students. A 1982 accreditation self-study report describes its present comprehensiveness:

Castile still draws a rather large portion of very able students. The school finds it must offer two to three sections of advanced placement work for all four years in English and three years in the social sciences. This year advanced placement sections are also offered in chemistry and mathematics. In addition, the school finds an increasing number of minority students enrolled and also increased numbers qualified as educationally handicapped. . . . For the first time, this school year, Castile qualifies as a Title I school and has been assigned a team of experts to aid in the new programs.

Castile's faculty members have accepted responsibility for these curricular changes; they assume that the task of improving teaching is a collective responsibility. As a group, they accept the obligation to serve student learning needs and to see curriculum development projects through. As a result, there is frequent talk about the practice of teaching and an opportunity to design and evaluate materials. One catalyst for this dialogue on important curricular issues is the weekly schedule. Meetings for faculty and students have a regular place on Wednesday mornings; then, in the first hour of the day, staffs, departments, clubs, or individuals meet to set policy, design activities, or discuss assignments.

Other than a supportive weekly schedule, which also includes an hour of released time daily for department heads, Castile teachers have typical material support for their work. They have generally large classes (thirty-nine students in history, thirty-eight in government, twenty-four in literature, and twenty-two in physics) grade their own student papers, perform their own clerical tasks, and teach a traditional five-class schedule. It is from this environment that the four teachers speak of their classroom and extra-classroom work.

The four, however, are not average teachers. They were selected for this study not for their representativeness but for the fact that they exhibit the different ways experienced secondary teachers think about content and instruction in making sense of their work of teaching critical thinking. Bob Post finds the central meaning of history in the power relationships among political, economic, and social forces; Conrad Rizzo in matter and energy.

Thus, both of them are concerned about key concepts from a single discipline. Linda Reed introduces principles from sociology, philosophy, and psychology into critical discussions of literature. Langdon Selhorst finds a similar coherence in historical and political principles for government. Both of them have integrated cross-disciplinary study into their understanding of subject matter. Whether chiefly concerned about one discipline or several, all four are involved in articulating that understanding for students and in developing that understanding through critical thinking. Yet, when each of them uses the moral discourse they share, they sometimes have difficulty in articulating the richness of their understanding. In the language they use, the coherence connecting their knowledge base with instructional processes and organizational processes sounds more fragmented and more intuitive than I found it in observations.

The common difficulty these four very able teachers have in explaining their content understanding is a characteristic problem of research on teacher thinking and of the education of teachers. For most of us, it is easier to think about what classroom activities and actions we wish to perform than, because of the complexities of classroom interactions, to know what exactly will be learned and how. Teachers are rarely invited to articulate their conceptions of subject matter, either in their professional education or as a part of their professional work. The main purpose of this study is to deepen our understanding of this often overlooked search by teachers to find a professional language that will articulate decisions earlier attributed to intuition and luck. It investigates the possibility of diagnosing the detailed knowledge base of teaching from the study of four teachers in action. It also highlights the resources our educational tradition provides—and fails to provide—for enabling us to think about the cognitive demands of teaching.

2

Cognition in Teaching

Heightened interest in research on teaching has revealed, among other things, the efficacy of direct instructional teacher behaviors, the importance of well-organized classrooms, and the complex relationship between time and learning. Until very recently, however, we have given little attention to the content of teaching—that is, the knowledge teachers teach students and how they communicate it effectively. As early as 1978, Fenstermacher (1978) called for inquiry into teachers' practical reasoning about teaching in specific situations. Only through such research, he argued, will we discover why teachers engage in effective practice. Writing in the *Handbook of Research on Teaching*, Shulman (1986a) describes this knowledge base for teaching as a "missing paradigm in research on teaching."

Although the literature on teacher thinking has investigated teachers' covert mental processes presumed to influence and guide professional action (Calderhead, 1986), most of this literature has used a generic rather than a contextual orientation. It has ignored subject matter influences upon teacher planning and decision making and, instead, has focused upon general strategies used by teachers across disciplines. In summarizing this research, Clark and Peterson (1986) affirm the importance of cognition in teaching, but note that the literature exhibits little of the coherence needed to transform it into a systematic cumulative body of research.

One problem, as Yinger (1986) has pointed out, is the restrictive nature of its primary characterization, the teacher as a decision maker. A decision-making model implies a linearity in intelligent behavior, but the general features of practical situations render this linearity impossible. Instead of working within highly rational situations, teachers design practical courses of action to serve the needs of a particular client group within situations that are complex, uncertain, unstable, unique, and contain value conflicts. Effective teaching is thus based on successful translation and adaptation of curricula into instructional activities suitable to diverse groups of students in idiosyncratic contexts. Teachers draw upon and successfully orchestrate tremendously large bodies of knowledge—subject matter, social knowledge, and pedagogical techniques—in this transformation.

Further, Confrey (1982) argues that the generic approach is inappropriate for studying secondary teaching. The subject matter orientation of secondary teachers requires different approaches to research on these teachers' knowledge base. Because the methods, processes, and strategies by which one comes to believe that something is warranted knowledge in a particular subject matter are a part of that knowledge, teacher thinking varies by subject matter orientation as well as by context. The manner in which a teacher portrays and teaches knowledge also reflects the values and social goals of a teacher.

This conception of teachers, promoted by Yinger and Confrey, is more inclusive than that of decision maker and incorporates a variety of activities, cognitive and social. It points to the increasingly central role played by well-educated teaching professionals in teaching reasoning. This role requires knowledge of rules and principles of critical thinking, knowledge of subject matter and pedagogy, and knowledge of the ways to transform and apply appropriate rules and subject matter in organizing particular classrooms for learning.

CHARACTERISTICS OF CRITICAL THINKING

One difficulty in discussing critical thinking stems from the lack of a common definition. In part, this difficulty is the result of a plethora of terms describing this cognitive activity. The process is variously referred to as reasoning (Glasman, Koff, and Spiers, 1984; Shulman and Carey, 1984), higher order thinking (Doyle, 1983; Sykes, 1985), intelligent behavior (Costa, n.d.), creative thinking (Keating, 1980), and thinking (Arendt, 1977), each with its own meaning. In part, this definitional difficulty is the result of changing pressures to shape literacy for socially productive ends. Historically, the meaning of literacy has changed from the ability to sign one's name to the ability to function in society to the ability to think critically (Clifford, 1984). These changes were motivated first by the need to read the Bible, then for patriotism and the assimilation of immigrants, then for economic improvement. Only since the Progressive Movement has reasoning been a part of our conception of literacy.

Nonetheless, the growth of concern about critical thinking has been, and continues to be, process specific and context dependent. Current definitions vary in their complexity and detail, but most focus on the outcomes of the cognitive processes involved. For example, one well-established definition of reasoning outlines four areas of activity:

• the ability to identify and formulate problems as well as the ability to propose and evaluate ways to solve them;
• the ability to recognize and use inductive and deductive reasoning and to recognize fallacies in reasoning;
• the ability to draw reasonable conclusions from information found in various sources (written, spoken, tables, graphs), and to defend one's conclusions rationally;
• the ability to distinguish between fact and opinion (Glasman, Koff, and Spiers, 1984, p. 467).

Another group defines higher order thinking as " 'active sustained cognitive effort directed at solving a complex problem', with a complex problem being one that requires a student to integrate different sources of information, consider alternative perspectives, make critical judgments, and develop and test the hypotheses" (Computers, 1985, p. 3). Costa (n.d.) promotes an information processing model of intellectual behavior composed of input, processing, and output; each element is composed of several cognitive processes. Keating (1980, pp. 57–58) describes the four components of creative thinking: (1) content knowledge—thorough familiarity with an accumulated base of knowledge/experience; (2) divergent thinking—the ability to entertain or generate new ideas easily from the knowledge base; (3) critical analysis—the ability to separate promising from unpromising avenues and to consider alternatives; and (4) communication skills—the ability to develop a product to be evaluated in a social content, outside the individual. Only Arendt (1977, p. 128) addresses the abstraction that must occur in the process of thinking: "Every thought is an afterthought. By repeating in imagination, we *re-sense* what has been given to our senses. And only in this immaterial form can our thinking faculty now begin to concern itself with these data. This operation preceeds all thought processes." During cognition, according to Arendt, all objects are subjected to a twofold transformation that readies a "sense object" as a suitable "thought object." For us to think about a thing, it must be removed from our presence.

These definitions, though varying in a number of elements, agree upon the complexity of the process and upon the abstraction needed for critical thinking. But the conception that communicates most clearly for teachers is that proposed by Doyle (1984a). He defines higher order processing skills, those requiring critical thinking, as the cognitive processes of comprehension, interpretation, flexible application of knowledge and skills, and assembly of information and resources. These higher order thinking processes produce new knowledge or knowledge in new forms; lower order processes reproduce knowledge from memory or through the application of routine. This is the definition that guided the classification of academic tasks from the observational data; I have, however, used the other terms as synonyms in this analysis.

Despite the disagreement over definition, and its resulting instruction, critical thinking is widely accepted as an important academic outcome for schools. As an illustration, in 1985 reasoning was included as one of fourteen resolutions adopted by the Association for Supervision and Curriculum Development (ASCD, 1985). Echoing the economic pressures Clifford (1984) identified, educators acknowledge that " participation in a changing and increasingly complex society requires citizens to process large amounts of information, sometimes to change careers and jobs, to relate with high sensitivity to others, and to operate effectively in ambiguous and unstructured situations. Such work demands thinking and thoughtful people" (p. 1). They also acknowledge that promoting student thinking skills requires careful planning if reasoning is to be practiced systematically and regularly.

In addition to Doyle's definition, the conception of critical thinking most influential in shaping this study is that summarized by Sykes (1985). The information processing perspective on intelligence, he notes, yields six important insights for the teaching of critical thinking.

First, academic tasks have incredible complexity. Here, for example, is one account of the composing process, one of the variety of academic tasks that promote higher order thinking:

As a cognitive activity, writing involves the use of specific kinds of knowledge that a writer has and is able to discover in constructing meanings and expressing them in writing. Underlying and enabling this use of knowledge are a variety of cognitive processes, including: discovering or generating an intended propositional meaning; selecting aspects of an intended propositional meaning; selecting aspects of an intended meaning to be expressed; choosing language forms that encode this meaning explicitly and, simultaneously, guide the reader/writer through different levels of comprehension; reviewing what has been written, and often revising to change and improve meaning and its expression (Frederiksen and Dominic, 1981, p. 2).

Although we are only beginning to understand this process, the importance of writing in thinking is attributed to the permanence of the written word, the explicitness required in writing, the resources provided by conventional forms of discourse, and the active nature of writing (Applebee, 1984). Because writing is integrative, available for review and reevaluation, connective, and active, recent research emphasizes its heuristic, problem-solving nature in writing about new material. This complexity, however, renders writing, like many critical thinking tasks, difficult to teach and difficult to learn. Nonetheless, the more students must manipulate materials in writing, the better they come to understand them.

Second, ill-structured tasks, the sort most frequently found in life, are absent in classrooms. "Instruction in problem solving usually emphasizes well-structured problems—the kind of problem which is clearly presented with all the information needed and with an appropriate algorithm available that guarantees a correct answer" (Frederiksen, 1984, p. 363). But important social, political, economic, and scientific problems seldom are so neatly structured. Teaching students to solve ill-structured problems would provide greater transfer of learning.

Third, we have differentiated the components of cognitive activity to include the skills of metacognition, performance, and knowledge acquisition used in problem solving. Armed with this knowledge, it is possible that we can increase the capacity for thinking through calling students' attention to metacognition, the executive skills by which individuals frame and monitor their own thought processes and activities. These executive skills are an important addition to procedures, algorithms, and propositional knowledge. To acquire executive skills in translating propositional knowledge into problem-solving procedures requires demonstration, models, explication, and more than the usual amount of practice (Frederiksen, 1984).

Fourth, the basic unit for developing higher order thinking is the task, which has three features: the product, the operations to be used to generate the product, and the resources available while generating the product. Each task can be categorized by the cognitive processes required to complete its product (Doyle, 1983). Some tasks, memory and procedural, require the reproduction of knowledge; others, comprehension and opinion, require the production of new knowledge, higher order thinking. Each requires different cognitive strategies for processing information. The memory task requires a student to memorize material and reproduce it accurately. In procedural or routine tasks students apply a formula to generate formulaic answers. The comprehension or understanding task requires students to understand and apply previous knowledge to problems, and make inferences and predictions. In opinion tasks students state preferences. Completing a task thus has two consequences. "First, a person will acquire information—facts, concepts, principles, solutions—involved in the particular task that is accomplished. Second, a person will practice operations—memorizing, classifying, inferring, analyzing—used to obtain or produce the information demanded in the task" (Doyle, 1983, p. 162). The cognitive skills students learn are dependent upon the tasks they are assigned.

Fifth, prior knowledge plays an important role in learning. Students already have preconceptions of the meaning of most new concepts that are presented in the classroom. "Thus learning and understanding do not mean the passive filling up of a container, but rather mean a restructuring of knowledge that is already present (Bromme, 1987, p. 139). Teaching requires not only the imparting of new content information but also the conveying of metaknowledge in such a way that it will restructure old ways of knowing.

Finally, cognitive abilities are specific to particular domains of knowledge. Although some (de Bono, 1983; Brown, 1983) argue for direct teaching of thinking as a separate skill, others (Mansfield, Busse, and Krepelka, 1978; Mansfield and Busse, 1982) have questioned the effectiveness of generic programs. Most current psychological research places thinking directly within the context of subject matter. McPeck (1981) affirms that thinking is always thinking about something. "Proposing to teach critical thinking in the abstract, in isolation from specific fields or problem areas, is muddled nonsense; thinking of any kind is always 'thinking about X' " (p. 13). Further, reasoning is the judicious use of skepticism supplied by the norms and standards of the field under consideration. It involves the skills necessary for engaging in an activity, and thinking cannot be divorced from the skills that make the activity what it is. "Insofar as critical thinking involves knowledge and skill, a critical thinker in area X might not be a critical thinker in area Y" (p. 13). Thus, critical thinking is not a frill added to one's education but is a logical part of it. Acceptable thinkers always think in context.

Based on these themes from research on cognition, the best approach in teaching reasoning is within the disciplinary areas of the curriculum. Teachers successful in training intellectual skills base their instruction on task analysis common to information processing models of intelligence, but they go beyond this (Wagner and Sternberg, 1984). They also base their instruction on task characteristics of intelligent behavior in the everyday world, directed toward metacognitive and cognitive levels and their interactions.

KNOWLEDGE BASE FOR TEACHING

Justification for an interest in the knowledge base for teaching is based on the assumption that teaching is a cognitive activity. This conception of teaching, argues Shulman (1987, p. 7), perhaps its most active advocate, has six commonplaces:

A teacher knows something not understood by others, presumably the students. The teacher can transform understanding, performance skills, or desired attitudes or values into pedagogical representations and actions. These are ways of talking, showing, enacting, or otherwise representing ideas so that the unknowing can come to know, those without understanding can comprehend and discern, and the unskilled can become adept. Thus, teaching necessarily begins with a teacher's understanding of what is to be learned and how it is to be taught. It proceeds through a series of activities during which the students are provided specific instruction and opportunities for learning, though the learning itself ultimately remains the responsibility of the students. Teaching ends with new comprehension by both the teacher and the student.

In this conception, teacher knowledge produces an inextricable link between teaching and subject matter, resulting in content-specific knowledge for teaching.

In the literature, references to teachers' knowledge and abilities appear under a number of different labels; all, however, make some reference to cognitive activity. They include such terms as perception, conception, development of knowledge structures, knowledge-in-action, and manipulation of ideas. This literature attempts to describe the meaning of what teachers do; the avenue currently taken is to begin with a teacher's point of view in order to develop an emerging set of notions about how to understand complex systems (Calfee, 1981).

To study teacher cognition, therefore, it is necessary to create a set of well-organized mental structures that parallel these covert processes that are the repository of teachers' own formal knowledge. Here, the image of the learner, the representation of a particular curriculum, principles for developing and selecting materials and activities, management, and moment-to-moment interactions form important components of structure. For example, Leinhardt (1986, p. 1) describes the complex cognitive skill of teaching as "(a) assembling known pieces of organized behaviors, namely, action systems, into effective sequences that meet particular goals; (b) assembling appropriate goals to meet larger teaching objectives, and (c) doing both in a way that attends to specific constraints in a total system." Byrne (1983) argues that the most relevant teacher knowledge for student achievement will be that which concerns both the particular topic being taught and the relevant pedagogical strategies for teaching it to the particular type of pupils to whom it will be taught.

In this literature, strong subject matter knowledge and effective strategies to transform this information into work tasks for students are seen as a primary cause of student achievement. In describing how physicians investigate and diagnose cases, Shulman (1974, p. 325) reached a similar conclusion:

It appears necessary to possess domain-specific knowledge to solve most problems. While the knowledge alone may not be sufficient in the absence of appropriate information-processing skills and a proper set of problem formulations, it is abundantly clear that no amount of general intellectual skill or mastery over cognitive strategies will overcome lacks in content knowledge. It seems reasonable to assume that a fairly complex set of knowledge by process interactions is involved in the construct we call clinical competence.

A background strong in subject matter and professional skills supports the conception of teachers as autonomous, self-directed professionals.

Until recently, however, teachers have not been seen as possessing a unique body of professional knowledge and expertise (Feiman-Nemser and

Floden, 1986). Instead, research has focused upon practical knowledge—insights, beliefs, and habits that enable teachers to do work in schools; this propositional knowledge, directly derived from descriptions of the way teaching is (Clark and Lampert, 1985), is situation specific, personally compelling, and oriented toward action. Clandinin (1985, 1986) takes this more individual view of teacher thinking, which she terms "personal practical knowledge." Personal practical knowledge is the mode of knowing used for everyday thinking. It is "experiential, embodied, and reconstructed out of the narratives of a user's life" (Connelly and Clandinin, 1985, p. 183). Because this knowledge is value-laden, purposeful, concerned with practice, tentative, and subject to change, it represents an effort to understand teachers within a framework of relations. The result is a unity in a particular person in a particular place and time of all past experiences and of the traditions that helped shape them. Elbaz (1983), in a similar study of the practical knowledge of one high school English teacher, identified the content of practical knowledge: knowledge of self, of the milieu of teaching, of subject matter, of curriculum development, and of instruction. This practical knowledge has five orientations: it is theoretical, situational, social, personal, and experiential. It is structured hierarchically by rules of practice, by practical principles, and by images.

Both Schon (1983) and Sockett (1987), writing more philosophically than empirically, argue for the inclusion of teacher reasoning in studies of teacher knowledge. Schon (1983) distinguishes between the active and reflective phases of professional life. "Knowledge-in-action" is his term for the knowledge apparent in a teacher's day-to-day actions. "Reflection-in-action" is a process in which teachers reframe practical problems in response to puzzles and surprises in order to solve them. Both, he argues, are a part of the knowledge base for teaching. Sockett (1987, p. 215) urges studies of teacher knowledge to include "reason in action—that which connects wisdom, tacit knowledge, plans, techniques, ideals, and justification within an experience." These elements meet as practice in the unpredictable, changing context of the classroom. Four studies have traced the growth of this professional knowledge in beginning teachers (Feiman-Nemser and Buchmann, 1986; Russell, 1986, 1987; Tamir, 1987).

Much of the work on the knowledge base for teaching, particularly pedagogical content knowledge and especially that held by secondary teachers, has come from the Knowledge Growth in Teaching project at Stanford University (Shulman, Sykes, and Phillips, 1983). Over a three-year period, including a year of professional education and two years of beginning teaching, this project has investigated how secondary teachers move from an understanding of a subject matter to transform that knowledge in forms of representation appropriate for students.

From this work, Shulman (1987, p. 8) and his colleagues have developed a conceptualization of the knowledge base for teaching that contains seven components:

—content knowledge;

—general pedagogical knowledge, with special reference to those broad principles and strategies of classroom management and organization that appear to transcend subject matter;

—curriculum knowledge, with particular grasp of the materials and programs that serve as "tools of the trade" for teachers;

—pedagogical content knowledge, that special amalgam of content and pedagogy that is uniquely the province of teachers, their own special form of professional understanding;

—knowledge of learners and their characteristics;

—knowledge of educational context, ranging from the workings of the group or classroom, the governance and financing of school districts, to the character of communities and cultures; and

—knowledge of educational ends, purposes, and values, and their philosophical and historical grounds.

The unique contribution of this conception is the notion of pedagogical content knowledge, that knowledge which permits transformation of content knowledge into forms of representation. This knowledge includes a repertoire of metaphors, analogies, and examples to convey this content as well as an understanding of student misconceptions of and difficulties with these concepts. It includes propositions for bringing teachers' other knowledge components to bear on this transformation. It involves knowledge not only of how—the capacity of skilled performance—but also of what and why. It permits professionals both to act and to communicate their reasoning in professional decisions and actions to others.

While making a major breakthrough in our understanding of teacher knowledge, Shulman's work is not without its critics, who have questioned the relationship among these components and the absence of teacher beliefs and personal qualities. Feiman-Nemser (1987) argues that this theory of teacher knowledge, or expertise, is too narrow. Additional components— particularly teacher beliefs and motivations, personal qualities, and dispositions toward teaching—need to be added. She argues, further, that the relations among components of this theory must be carefully considered. In her work with elementary teachers at Michigan State University, she separates a teacher's personal knowledge of a subject from ideas of what good teaching is. An orientation to subject matter contains teachers' knowledge of the nature of subject matter and their knowledge of how one does subject matter—their understanding of English, or history, or mathematics. These ideas are analytically separated from the orientation to presentation, which includes pedagogical knowledge and teacher beliefs about what good English—or history, biology, or mathematics—teaching is. This, Feiman-Nemser shows, is necessary for understanding each category and for establishing standards for judging the appropriateness of teacher beliefs. Similarly, Byrne (1983) argues that interactive teaching is shaped by a teacher's plan, which embodies and reflects the teacher's intentions, knowledge, and beliefs about what should be taught and how it should be taught. Yinger (1986) also includes "knowledge of self" as one of five basic types of knowledge that influence teacher practice. Sockett (1987) suggests that Shulman pays too little attention to the influence of context upon teaching. Teaching, Sockett asserts, involves complex judgments of balance between ideal and possible practice, not merely pure pedagogical reasoning. What is good teaching is always the result of practical judgment, rooted in context. Richardson-Koehler (1987) calls for further study of the relationship between teacher orientation and belief and classroom action.

Nonetheless, Shulman reminds us that teachers' specific knowledge of subject matter is the result of their prior knowledge of content and of pedagogical knowledge that shapes the ways in which that content is taught. Each discipline identifies skills a curriculum might impart: skills by which one applies the truths learned from a discipline; skills of enquiry itself; skills of reading and interpretation by which one discovers the meaning of statements that are embedded in a context of structure. Which of these skills we teach will determine what our students learn (Schwab, 1978a). This orientation to subject matter encompasses both knowledge of the various ways a discipline can be organized or understood (Knitter, 1987) and understanding of the ways by which a discipline evaluates and accepts new knowledge. Schwab (1978b, p. 246) refers to these as the substantive, "the conceptual devices which are used for defining, bounding, and analyzing the subject matters they investigate," and the syntactic, "the different methods of verification and justification of conclusions."

Based upon these structures, teachers sometimes organize their conceptions of subject matter through a variety of models, metaphors, or images. The selection of a metaphor appears to perform two functions. It is, first of all, a means for making public a teacher's understanding. Holton (1984, p. 112) notes that metaphors can act "sometimes as a means for the transfer of meaning across discontinuity, as a bridge or a boat is a means for transferring a person across a river." Arendt (1977, p. 146) calls this bridge for the gap between invisible mental activities and the world of appearances "the greatest gift that language can bestow on thinking." The selection of a metaphor thus determines a perspective or frame (Schon, 1979). But metaphors have a second purpose. They suggest ways to act or solve problems. To view an urban area as a blight rather than a redevelopment calls a different set of actions into play. Metaphors are, therefore, "a process by which new perspectives on the world come into existence" (Schon, 1979,

p. 254). They are "a more active tool of metamorphosis, or a restructuring of a portion of the world view" (Holton, 1984, p. 112). Elbaz (1983, p. 148) notes that "imagery is a generalization from practical rules and principles to a metaphorical form of guidance for action." This language, vital to professional thinking, generates the problem and how one imagines its solution (Schon, 1979). Images thus mediate between thought and action, express teachers' purposes, guide them intuitively, determine action, and extend knowledge.

A few studies have offered the conceptualization of image as a central construct for understanding teacher knowledge and for linking such knowledge to past experiences and to ongoing practical expressions. Munby (1986) identified the occurrence and significance of metaphors in teachers' accounts of their practical knowledge with their ways of interpreting classroom events and awareness of possible alternative interpretations. An image is a personal meta-level organizing concept in a teacher's knowledge; it embodies a perspective from which new experience is taken. It also provides cues to the congruence or incongruence between teachers' espoused theories and theories in action (Munby, 1985). Clandinin (1986) found that these images function both to represent a teacher's philosophy and to direct action in coping with classroom situations. Actions and practices then become expressions of images. Morine-Dershimer (1984), in an analysis of transcripts from stimulated recall, noticed that teachers differ in the imagery they use to discuss classroom events. These images—battle, entertainment, headlong movement, housewife, confrontation, and avoidance—give clues to implicit teacher beliefs.

Further, the effectiveness of metaphors and models to communicate content and guide action is based upon the extent to which the organizing imagery is appropriate and beneficial to students. Based upon comparison, a metaphor can represent pedagogical content knowledge in a particularly striking way. It does render the incomprehensible more accessible. As such it is a useful vehicle for pedagogical thinking. But the main liability of using metaphors is that they "do not carry with them clear demarcations of the areas of their legitimacy. They may be effective tools for [teachers], but pathetic fallacies for students" (Holton, 1984, p. 102) unless teachers address the cultural differences between teacher and student. Metaphors communicate differently to individuals with different experiences. For example, the metaphor of space represents infinity to a scientist but a place where birds fly to a child. Teachers need to be aware of the "metaphoric *distance* between [themselves] and [their] colleagues on the one hand and [their] students on the other; to be aware of the metaphoric *dissonance* that reverberates strongly, even though unattended, in every classroom" (p. 110).

Pedagogical content knowledge, in addition to embodying subject knowledge, also concerns the teacher's capacity for representing the knowledge being taught (Byrne, 1983). Byrne (p. 18) proposes that it is this representation that principally dfferentiates the more effective from the less effective teacher in knowledge of subject matter:

Effective teaching, I suggest, consists of the teacher employing appropriate representations—representations which in some way relate to, or build upon, the representations of knowledge which pupils already possess. Effective teaching also involves gradually moving pupils through different representations of the same concept, or conceptual net. It usually starts with the concrete or familiar . . . but later this is discarded in the course of the pupils' acquisition of the more abstract and purely conceptual knowledge which is the aim of instruction.

Byrne's forms of representations, moving from the concrete to the abstract, are similar to the enactive, the iconic, and the symbolic modes of representation first proposed by Bruner (1971).

These forms of representations are "devices that humans use to make public conceptions that are privately held" (Eisner, 1982, p. 47). Teachers need to find ways of representing concepts that match the representations students already possess. These representations require thought about "how to build bridges between one's own understanding and that of one's students" (Feiman-Nemser & Buchmann, 1986, p. 239). In order to build these bridges, a teacher's pedagogical thinking must be grounded in more than understanding of subject matter; it also requires understanding of students and self. This pedagogical thinking enables experienced teachers to attend to concepts and to students and to what in these concepts needs explaining to these students. To explain, teachers must be able to step outside the topic, to have command of the technical language for describing subject matter, a structural framework for organizing the details, and a grounded set of experiences related to the topic (Calfee, 1986).

Only a few studies have focused upon the pedagogical content knowledge of teachers in particular disciplines. Baxter, Richert, and Saylor (1985) studied beginning biology teachers and found, in a small sample, a high level of education in biology and independent study experiences associated with a complexity of relationships among concepts and of approaches to teaching; these biology teachers tend to approach topics from the general to the specific. Lower levels of content background were more associated with a view of inquiry as a set of prescribed techniques, a conception of simpler relationships within a field, and a focus on specific information in teaching. In a study comparing English majors and English education majors, Clift and Morgan (1986) found the two groups' pedagogical content knowledge contained three areas of difference: (1) the existence of fixed and fluid concepts in organization of the field of English, (2) the role of authority in interpreting literature and evaluating writing, and (3) the implicit model of learners in the classrooms. Majors valued depth of knowledge, teachers the breadth of knowledge. Teachers had a different purpose in reading and analyzing literature for teaching than the literature majors. In another study, Grossman, Reynolds, Ringstaff, and Sykes (1985) found that as students, prospective English teachers embraced three orientations to literature: to the text, to content, and to the reader. Once teaching is begun, however, these beginning teachers distinguished between their approaches as students and as teachers. Most, but not all, shifted toward the reader-centered approach. One study of two expert English teachers (Gudmundsdottir, 1987b) shows how this scholarly background becomes the foundation for restructuring content knowledge for pedagogical purposes. These two teachers generate models that effectively transmit their views of the discipline to their students. In social science, Gudmundsdottir, Carey, and Wilson (1985) found that prior knowledge influences the way beginning social studies teachers organize and teach their classes. These teachers draw on the particular aspect of their discipline—history, political science, or sociology—that has been important to them in their own education. Since the multiple structures of the social science disciplines produce multiple approaches to scholarship and teaching, teaching social studies differs among individuals and disciplines. Gudmundsdottir (1987a) traces through two case studies the transformation of two anthropology majors into high school social studies teachers, as they shift from a single disciplinary orientation to an interdisciplinary one. In a case study of beginning secondary social studies teachers, Wilson and Wineburg (1987) show how teacher belief influences action. In these teachers, knowledge of subject matter was a product not only of prior training and the accumulation of facts and interpretations gained through teaching, but also a product of beliefs; the information newly learned in teaching was often shaped by older, inaccurate information and, unless challenged, fundamental beliefs went unchanged.

From this work we know that a teacher's behavior cannot be properly understood without an appreciation of the teacher's knowledge, thinking, and intentions. Particular bits of behavior take their meaning from the teacher's overall knowledge base. Focusing attention on teacher behavior without attending to the teacher's strategy or intention can lead, at best, to a very limited understanding of teaching. If our task is a full understanding, we must consider the teacher knowledge, particularly pedagogical content knowledge, as well as classroom performance.

CLASSROOM ORGANIZATION AND MANAGEMENT

Recent research on effective teaching has identified an important relationship between time and learning. Students learn more when opportunities for learning increase, when they are actively engaged in activities, and when they are relatively successful in solving the problems presented (Denham and Lieberman, 1980). While making a significant contribution to our understanding of classroom processes, this research is based on the fundamental assumption that students willingly cooperate in activities provided in the allotted time. But student cooperation does not exist a priori in classrooms. Its presence, or absence, is the result of a teacher's skill in securing and sustaining that cooperation.

Earlier research on classroom management is based on a linear ends-means conception of teaching. Written lesson plans with goals and outcomes specified to direct the teaching have been used in these studies as a means to understand the teacher's skills. The planning models (Tyler, 1949; Popham and Baker, 1970) that influence this way of looking at teacher skills assume a rational, predictable environment. These researchers believe that if a teacher specifies objectives, selects learning activities, organizes learning activities, and specifies evaluation procedures in a neat orderly fashion, the lesson will proceed smoothly. Teaching is viewed as progressing, just as the teacher's plans state, in a logical way from the stated goals.

However, recent research on teacher thinking has documented that this is not the case. Instead, teachers have a lesson framework in mind and design it as they teach. The interactive classroom provides information and teachers are responsive to it while teaching. In the course of teaching, they may pick up cues from the classroom, indicating that something is going wrong. During the majority of these times, they may elect to go on with the lesson rather than respond to the cue. At other times, they choose to respond and then their thinking is more improvisational. This swift pace of the interaction often precludes a rational choice between limited alternatives. Instead, the skills required are flexibility and negotiation in a fluid classroom. This negotiation in the bargaining process is functional. It provides classroom cohesion by letting the participants create work and work arrangements that are specific to their needs and situation (Dillard, 1987).

Thus, to understand cognition in classrooms requires a situational approach based on interpreting thought and action in a particular setting—to consider the events surrounding the participants, the configurations of events over time, and the tasks themselves (Doyle, 1979a, 1986). "Thus, the types of activities a teacher uses are closely associated with the character of order in a class" (Carter, 1986, p. 19). In short, to understand the knowledge base for teaching critical thinking also requires consideration of the ways classrooms are organized and managed.

To focus upon classroom organization means a focus upon the tasks assigned to students. A number of studies have followed this approach (Anderson, Evertson, and Emmer, 1982; Brophy, 1983; Brophy and Putnam, 1978; Kounin, 1970), but it has been Doyle's work (1977, 1979b, 1983, 1984a, 1985, 1986) that has articulated it most consistently. A task is the way in which information processing demands of an environment are structured and experienced. It shapes the way information is selected and processed, and it is the fundamental organizer of behavior in settings. Classroom tasks "designate the situational structures that organize and direct thought and action" (Doyle and Carter, 1984, p. 130). Students seek information, work to redefine tasks, and accept additional information as a part of their performance. "Tasks are not simply imposed or provided by some outside force. Rather people have to define them, formulate goals for them, determine their relevant constraints, and identify resources available in the setting" (Nespor, 1987, p. 204). Completing such a task consists in part of discovering, creating, or interpreting goals, operations, and constraints. Thus, different student performances may stem from differences in knowledge and effort or from different understandings and definitions of the task.

A teacher's responsibility, then, is to create work settings that promote and support learning. These management decisions are rooted in cognition. As Doyle (1986, p. 424) states, "the key to a teacher's success in management appears to be his or her (a) understanding of the likely configuration of events in the classroom, and (b) skill in monitoring and guiding activities in light of this information." For teachers, creating an environment conducive to learning involves two types of pedagogical decisions: those designed to capture student attention and interest in subject matter, and those that monitor and pace activities in order to maintain interest throughout the school year. Doyle (1979a, p. 47) refers to these decisions as those that "gain and maintain cooperation in classroom activities."

Here, "cooperation" refers to a wide variety of student behaviors that are appropriate to a particular task and teacher expectation.

Cooperation is not a euphemism for compliance or control, although these latter terms may define cooperation in a particular setting. Neither is cooperation equivalent to involvement, since passivity (that is, willingness to go along with or at least not disrupt an activity) can under certain circumstances be a sufficient level of cooperation for some of the students in a classroom. Further, norms of rationality that specify appropriate classroom activities differ across settings and teachers vary their tolerances for modes of student conduct (Doyle, 1979a, p. 47).

In different classrooms, cooperation may be exhibited in talk or silence, in sitting quietly or working aimlessly, in interrupting or waiting. It refers to a student's willingness to participate, even passively, in an activity.

Two structural features of student work tasks exacerbate a teacher's role in managing critical thinking tasks. Academic tasks and classroom activities exist within a context of ambiguity and risk (Doyle, 1979b). Ambiguity refers here not to a poorly designed assignment, but to the uncertainty surrounding the selection of appropriate cognitive procedures and to the vagueness of the standards for judgment. Some tasks, such as objective tests, because they call upon the retrieval of information from memory or routine and have highly certain evaluation criteria, are low in ambiguity. Higher order thinking tasks, such a essays, are much more ambiguous: The task does not prescribe particular ideas to use, an appropriate organizing structure, a sense of adequate development, or the logical relation of ideas; and the criteria for effectiveness are less predictable.

To complete a learning task, students must be able to display a capability that does not presently exist. This accountability includes both a summative evaluation of products and public recognition of students' efforts. In order to perform successfully, they must bridge gaps between their understanding and the product to be produced by processing information (Doyle, 1983). The wider the gap is between the known and the unknown, the greater the student's risk of failure. Because some tasks call upon known information or procedures, the amount of needed learning is small and the risk low. Critical thinking tasks, however, require large amounts of new learning and, as such, carry greater risk of failure. It is the ambiguous and risky nature of critical thinking tasks that makes them more difficult for teachers to manage in classrooms (Doyle, Sanford, Clements, Schmidt French, and Emmer, 1983). "The more complex a program of action for an activity, the more difficult a management task a teacher faces" (Doyle, 1986, p. 424). Thus, structural features of academic tasks place specialized demands upon interactive skills of teachers.

Participating in academic tasks, however, does not remain constant once students have agreed to cooperate. Teachers must also monitor levels of participation, sustain interest, and synchronize their goals with student concerns. The real job for students in classrooms, therefore, is to be able to behave appropriately when their competence is judged. Students thus try to accomplish classroom tasks in ways that reduce ambiguity and/or risk. In all tasks and activities, students push for predictability—their work is more understandable when stringent evaluation criteria are available. During critical thinking tasks, those requiring the production rather than the reproduction of information, this synchronization frequently requires coordinating the press between student self-direction and order in the classroom (Doyle and Carter, 1987).

Teachers respond to this press in a variety of ways. Most negotiate with students. Dillard (1987) identifies these instances of press as "bargaining" that is initiated either by teachers or students. Bargaining, like lessons, concerns work and involves negotiation and haggling. But in a bargain, the goal is more specific than a discussion of literary theme or rules of usage. Instead, bargains are negotiated over "(1) the amount of time students will have to complete assignments, (2) the number of parts needed for satisfactory work, (3) whether or not the assignment merits extra credit, and (4) the procedure the work will involve" (p. 7). The teacher's major goals embedded in bargaining actions are coordinating the social system, motivating learners, gathering knowledge, assessing knowledge, providing information, providing practice, and creating fun. This bargaining makes the classroom a more interesting place for both teacher and students, sharpens the relationship between the two, builds community, and serves as a functional teaching strategy. Lampert's (1985) case study of teachers managing conflict has some findings similar to Dillard's work. Lampert refers to situations like the bargaining occasions as "dilemmas." In her study, conflict is not seen as a negative but as a continuing classroom condition. The teachers accept conflict as useful because of its ability to empower their teaching. These occasions are special opportunities that help teachers to be more inventive and make their teaching more powerful. Finally, as Nespor (1987) suggests, even evaluation can be an opportunity for negotiation. Occasionally, an assessment of a completed task may clarify the task goal, identify unrecognized resources, and elaborate connections between goals and procedures. In this sense, tasks can receive retrospective interpretation and can be transformed after the fact.

The task of securing and sustaining student cooperation is, therefore, a key component of all classrooms, regardless of the discipline or experience of the teacher. In the course of this bargaining or sustaining student cooperation, however, teachers may unintentionally reduce the cognitive demands of critical thinking tasks—by managing time and content of recitation, by changing the degrees of ambiguity and risk involved in the task structure itself, by increasing prompts and decreasing the processing load, or by reducing the extent learning is necessary to accomplish this task. Two studies of secondary education have documented this reduction. Doyle and Carter (1984) found a junior high teacher had only limited success in engaging students in the composing process. There, the tension between "the teacher's emphasis on latitude for exercising composing skills and the students' concern for guidance and predictability in an evaluative situation" (p. 146) rendered these higher level tasks unstable. In a study of six junior high teachers, Sanford (1985) found that teachers reduced cognitive demands by providing extra credit, allowing revision for an improved grade, establishing less exacting standards for low-ability students, and grading some minor tasks on effort and completion rather than accuracy. All found it difficult to sustain the cognitive challenges of reasoning tasks. Managing this press is hard work, for all teachers.

This cognitive approach to classroom organization suggests that a teacher's fundamental management task is establishing workable systems for classroom groups rather than identifying and extinguishing misbehavior or motivating student engagement. The task is order, not discipline. This approach also highlights the critical role of classroom interaction in learning: What students learn is a direct product of this teacher/student interaction. Thus, this approach emphasizes the fundamental tension between organizational and instructional processes in the classroom and implies its significance for student achievement.

SUMMARY

From this review of the literature on critical thinking, on the knowledge base for teaching, and on classroom organization and management, I have drawn three principles that have informed this study. First, the process of critical thinking is highly complex, varied, and embedded in subject matter; how students process information is discovered in the academic tasks they are assigned and complete. Second, since learning to reason is content dependent, then an understanding of how teachers understand subject matter is critical to understanding how teachers teach critical thinking. This understanding of teacher knowledge would especially attend to a teacher's pedagogical content knowledge but also to teacher beliefs, knowledge of students, and knowledge of curriculum. Third, because structural features of tasks influence the relative difficulty or ease in organizing and managing student performance on these tasks, a study of teaching critical thinking must also attend to classroom interactions during instruction. Ordering the press between teacher goals and student self-direction is an important feature of this process. These principles direct the analysis of the work of four expert teachers found in Chapters 3, 4, and 5.

3

Teacher Knowledge for Teaching Critical Thinking

In order to develop critical thinking skills in students, teachers need a broad and deep understanding of subject matter and an understanding of the pedagogical strategies needed to transform and make public that understanding. This subject matter understanding, in experienced teachers like Bob, Langdon, Linda, and Conrad, encompasses both knowledge about how their discipline is organized and understood and knowledge of the ways by which their discipline evaluates and accepts new knowledge. Their pedagogical thinking enables them to attend to concepts and to students and to what in these concepts needs explaining to these students. In addition, their beliefs about good teaching and their dispositions toward action influence decisions about content. Drawn from these understandings, an organizing imagery fuses relations among major segments of this knowledge; it is a means of shaping decisions about what to teach and how to teach it.

SUBJECT MATTER KNOWLEDGE

Two domains of structure dominate these teachers' orientation to subject matter: structures related to knowledge of the nature of subject matter, and structures related to how one verifies or produces knowledge in that discipline. In discussing the disciplinary content of their teaching, for example, Bob, Langdon, Linda, and Conrad stress fundamental concepts of history, government, literature, and physics. They also stress the importance of reading, writing, and problem solving to an understanding of that subject matter. While all four teachers direct their courses entirely or predominantly toward these cognitive goals, they differ in their selection of content structures and analytical skills.

Thinking About Power. Bob places power—particularly social, economic, and political power—at the center of the game of historical study. His course syllabus for U.S. History-Honors reads:

This course will focus considerable time on concepts that both help us understand early American history and develop generalizations that have powerful applicability beyond the original historical context. These concepts should become intellectual tools that help one make sense of other historical periods as well as contemporary society. We will make frequent efforts to seek relationships between the past and the present and I urge, therefore, that you regularly focus on current events in the media.

The concept of *power* will be the central semester focus. Most other key concepts will relate in either a direct or indirect way to conflicts surrounding the creation, location, use, and abuse of social, economic, and especially political power.

His course preview also lists four themes that organize the content of early American history: the creation of the American culture, the clash of colonial empires, the internal revolution, and the creation of a new nation. These themes help him to select historical events for study. Each event is interpreted through a variety of philosophical positions. In early American history, for example, the two dominant but conflicting conceptions of power are most clearly articulated by Jefferson and Hamilton. Both positions carry social, political, and economic consequences for historical and contemporary contexts.

To develop an understanding of this concept of history, Bob uses the skills of reading, writing, thinking, and, to a much lesser extent, oral presentation. These are described in his course preview and in interviews. His syllabus explicitly names three reading skills that increase historical understanding.

a. Using the textbook to learn basic content.

b. Detecting biases and weaknesses of textbook history.

c. Identifying the main ideas and argument structures of conflicting historical interpretations. (There will be frequent outside readings which will require careful—sometimes painful—analysis.)

Indicating those elements in critical reading that are to be developed in the course of the semester, Bob identifies the text as a source of information, shaped by a point of view and interpretation. Parenthetically, he suggests that critical reading is hard work.

Writing is also used to increase historical understanding. In particular, Bob focuses upon five kinds of writing skills:

a. Organizing descriptions of events and periods of history.

b. Comparing different historical events, forces, periods, or individuals.

c. Analyzing causation.

d. Creating metaphors to probe meaning and explore relationships.

e. Synthesizing primary source data in preparation for document-based question exams.

Writing is a way to organize thought, to point out similarities and differences in events and historical periods, to trace the relation between cause and effect, to break through stereotypic ways of thinking, and to assemble information from various resources for document-based questions. Moreover, writing is important "to communicate clearly." These writing strategies and their relation to an understanding of historical principles, like the treatment of reading skills, are precise and clear.

Reasoning skills, inherent both in the components of reading and of writing, are also a part of discussion. In explaining his goals for students, he begins: "I like to get the kids thinking"; then he elaborates upon ways to foster reasoning in the classroom. He focuses upon the shaping of assignments and the classroom environment necessary to build critical skills. "I think a major problem in [encouraging reasoning] is to create thinking problems where kids don't see the answer as a simple one." In discussion, he emphasizes the logic in statements, seeking a justification and explanation of answers. "I ask questions and attack student answers." His classroom climate supports this active inquiry: "I like my classroom to be informal, friendly, demanding. Not chaos or even borderline chaos but active. So I tend to have students pushing me farther than I'd like." This lively oral activity is based on Bob's belief in the ownership of ideas that is built first orally and later in writing. "I'm also interested in oral presentation, not formal presentations but the oral expression of ideas. I believe we own ideas we express, and not just in writing."

Bob's definition of the substance of history is clear; like the beginning history teachers in Gudmundsdottir, Carey and Wilson's study (1985), the structural relations of concepts are dynamic and drawn from his prior knowledge as a historian. Bob's orientation to subject matter is based upon understanding of content and an approach that emphasizes values and perspectives, one of five major approaches to the teaching of history (Hazlett, 1987). He emphasizes the morality of historical study rather than facts, historiography, or the genesis of current events.

Preparing Rational Citizens. A moral goal for Langdon's American government class is an understanding of the governmental concepts needed for an informed citizenry. For the nature of these concepts and their substance, Langdon relies upon the hierarchical structure found in a district statement of student competencies for American government. Goal 2, for example, "basic principles," is divided into "democratic principles," "Constitutional principles," "legal principles," and "governmental principles espoused by major political groups." Goal 5, "the electoral process and political parties," is divided into "terms," "functions of national politics," and "election of public officials." As Castile High School's representative on the district curriculum committee, he helped shape this proposed list of eleven goals and their component parts.

Langdon communicates these goal statements to his students primarily through a description of four major units. His course outline issues, first, a general statement of goals: "This course [develops an] understanding of structure, function, and process of government as one of the basic foundations of citizenship in a participatory democracy." This goal is further defined as a "basic knowledge about political science as it relates to American government" and "basic skills in advocacy." The four major topics for the semester—The American Plan of Government, The Bill of Rights, The Political Spectrum and Political Parties, and The California Plan of Government—are of equal importance, each lasting three weeks; each follows logically and sequentially from the other. Within the narrative descriptions of these units, major concepts and their relations are suggested. For example, the description of Unit 1–The American Plan of Government suggests the tension among major concepts of power and governance:

The major emphasis of this unit, however, is on the analysis of the U.S. Constitution and Amendments in action. After studying the principles of separation of powers, checks and balances, and federalism, attention will be focused on the structures and operation of the legislative, executive, and judicial branches of the federal government with some emphasis given to the dynamic relationship among all three branches as they attempt to deal with crucial problems facing American society.

Relations among the three branches are transactional and reciprocal; their multiple connections alter future relations in subtle and complex ways.

For Langdon, the substance of political science is a set of overlapping topics and concepts of sometimes simple and sometimes complex relations, as represented in the district competencies. It is an understanding of the structure, function, and process of government as represented in the course's four required units. And finally, it is a spectrum of political values that are continually in conflict. In each unit, Langdon's prior knowledge of social science and his training as a lawyer have colored and infused this understanding of the structure of political science. Similar phenomena have been found among beginning social science teachers (Gudmundsdottir et al., 1985).

To verify and justify understanding of these concepts, Langdon promotes skills in writing, thinking, and critical reading. His course outline identifies the importance of composing skills to an understanding of political and governmental institutions: "First, we are committed to emphasizing the development of excellent writing skills, because we believe that good training in the written word leads to careful, thoughtful analyses of the value-loaded problems we study in American Government." His students are encouraged to record their ideas clearly in writing and to support their assertions with evidence from the resources provided. The debate inherent in these assertions is sometimes also present in the wording of written assignments:

Assume that in the contemporary world there is a battle for men's minds as it relates to the quest for "the good society," and identify, if you can, a political system or ethic which you would kill or die for in the battle for the minds of Man.

Reasoning is developed through weekly writing assignments, such as this one, as well as through discussion. The course outline identifies this second goal: "Students will be encouraged to think for themselves and to develop their own political values, party, or interest group affiliation and philosophical orientation." Langdon believes strongly in the importance of critical thought. He teaches independent thinking through reading multiple political perspectives. In addition, by confronting ideas in a meaningful and immediate way, he works to wean students from their dependence upon parents and teachers as sources of political truth.

A further goal, related to writing and thinking, is critical reading. In his initial interview, Langdon stressed the importance of developing students' interpretive and analytical skills in reading. He promotes this skill through active involvement with primary sources and discussion. Early in the semester, the discussions of the Declaration of Independence and the Constitution establish his expectations for careful, close reading. Later reading of sections from *The Brothers Karamazov* and *Das Kapital* reinforce these skills.

Like Bob, Langdon believes in the reciprocal relation among reading, writing, and thinking. Thinking in combination with other skills develops and strengthens all three: Critical reading and thinking provide the content for writing; writing and thinking further develop interpretations of reading.

Accomplishing these course goals requires concentrated effort and hard work and carries a particular ideology. Here, Langdon is quite direct in expressing the discipline required for success. His course outline reads: "We hope to help our students discover the joy of learning, even it if is often accomplished through long hours of study, rigorous academic challenge, and painful self evaluation." The intellectual conflict of this struggle is designed to promote specific political values. He works to develop his students' faith in the American system of government: Like Churchill, he believes that "democracy is the worst kind of government, except for all the rest," and hopes to instill that belief in his students. His course outline describes the component understandings and skills of this position:

It is our professional concern and commitment, therefore, that students we graduate leave us with experience that will foster good citizenship, that they have acquired basic knowledge about political science as it relates to American government, that they have begun to develop basic skills in advocacy and critical thinking, and that they have begun to consciously formulate appropriate values and attitudes preparatory to participation in our political and governmental institutions.

Langdon's orientation to subject matter is less unified than Bob's. Concepts of a democratic form of government are developed in four units through comparison to other political systems. Critical understanding of these ideas are developed through writing and reading. Like Bob, however, his approach stresses the values inherent in these principles.

Reading Critically. Linda's goals for students are particular to specific literature and literary skills. The course prospectus for Senior Seminar/AP names topics and materials for study. Hers is primarily a course in literary criticism in which students read such advanced works of drama, poetry, and fiction as *The American, Crime and Punishment, Sons and Lovers,* and *King Lear.* Literary knowledge is organized within these genres and the sources of evidence for interpretation exist within the texts themselves. Furthermore, the course is "designed to prepare students to pass the Advanced Placement Examination in English given each spring." A secondary goal is an understanding of concepts drawn from fields other than literature that are discussed by major literary figures and literary critics. Her syllabus reads:

The course is a philosophy, psychology, aesthetics and sociology course in that students will be reading not only the ideas of some of the world's greatest writers but also will be reading literary criticism which demands of them critical thinking about ideas in the novels as well as about the techniques of the novelists.

For Linda, the analytical skills necessary to the study of literature are skillful reading, composing, and literary analysis. She draws her reading goals from statements published by the Advanced Placement Program of the College Board:

The goal of a course in literature might well be to transform ordinary readers who understand English into informed, experienced, and critical readers, people whose understanding of the text derives from their sensitivity to its art and their ability to deal intelligently with all its elements (Jones and Wimmers, n.d., p. 1).

Literary analysis thus requires close and skillful reading of the novels named in the course prospectus; careful analysis is impossible without such reading.

Linda also defines the relation of composition to the study of literature: "Students will refine their writing skills, especially the writing of the thesis essay, reviewing sentence structure and punctuation as tools to help them better understand other writers' style and improve their own written style as well." Here she has incorporated, in a more general way, a statement from the Advanced Placement materials:

Developing a critical essay is in many ways a better test of a student's ability to respond to literature and to analyze the features of a particular work. For in writing an essay, a student must ask questions of the text as well as answer them, and he or she is also free to comment on the nuances, ambiguities, and contradictions that make the reading of literature such an interesting experience (Jones and Wimmers, n.d., p. 3).

Although Linda's written statement focuses upon the organizational structures of effective writing rather than on composition's role in understanding literature, she teaches writing as both a process and a means to develop thought.

Like her treatment of reading skills, Linda's description of the skills of literary analysis is inherent in her course materials and interview data. She clearly intends students to analyze the language, structure, and meaning of literary texts. The application of literary terminology is one means to this end:

AP students have been learning key literary terms during their preceding years. These terms will be reviewed and the list added to, particularly with poetry terms. The most important part of this study is *not* the memorization of definitions but, rather, the student's ability to use the term correctly when analyzing literature or poetry.

Literary terms are important tools of analysis rather than ends in themselves.

For Linda, the field of literature is fundamentally an understanding of the text, using the traditional tools of literary analysis to uncover meaning. It is, secondarily, a world of ideas drawn from other disciplines that mediate an understanding of literature. Thus, Linda has two differing conceptions of the structure of literature, a "text-centered orientation" and a "context-centered orientation" (Grossman et al., 1985). Although the reader-centered approach is most common in high school English classes, a conceptual structure centered on the text is equally appropriate for this Advanced Placement Senior Seminar: While it is not the the most prevalent approach to literature found in secondary English departments, it is the orientation of AP examiners and is the chosen orientation for experienced readers. Linda's dual conception may also be the result of contextual features of this year. Although a highly experienced teacher, this is her first year at Castile and she has not built a library of specific literature for this course; in subsequent years she may place much greater emphasis upon particular texts.

Solving Problems. In listing his goals for students, Conrad names an introduction to the major concepts of physics as one of his three central concerns. But his understanding of the structure of his discipline is defined by time. On his syllabus for Physics 1–2, a year-long course, each of the eighteen units focuses upon one concept, following the text for the course. These concepts are placed into an informal hierarchy by the allocation of time. Moreover, since instructional time is finite, the time devoted to each topic suggests its weighted importance. Physical concepts that are most fundamental, those receiving the most time, were "rectilinear motion," "curvilinear motion," and "the nature of light." Next in importance are "force," "kinetic theory of matter," "thermal effects," "wave motion," "reflection," "refraction," and "diffraction and polarization." Of modest importance are "measurement," "work, power, and energy," "heat and work," "electrostatics," and "direct current circuits." Receiving the least allocated time are "sound waves" and "heating and chemical effects." This time system identifies levels of importance and priority but leaves fluid the relations of concepts within each rating category.

Underlying this time structure are two fundamental concepts: matter and energy. These are not assigned a time sequence but are embedded within the explanation of individual units. The description of the first unit, for example, reads: "In the first chapter of the text you will be introduced to some terminology which we will be using throughout the course which is related to the fundamental concepts of matter and energy." These concepts, in addition to being fundamental, have mysterious qualities. Conrad's syllabus description of the first of four chapters on light suggests both their known and unknown features.

The Nature of Light. This chapter introduces the two theories about the nature of light—corpuscular and wave theory. It discusses the electromagnetic spectrum, introduces the photoelectric effect, and treats the quantum theory. It is a confusing chapter at times because we are not certain today which of the theories is "right." This is not a bad thing—no science student should leave thinking we know all there is to know.

Another chapter emphasizes light's behavior and use. "Diffraction and Polarization. In this chapter you will learn how the behavior of light as it passes through slits and around corners has been used as an analytical tool by science for exploring the earth and the extra-terrestrial universe."

Two interrelated scientific methods are necessary to analyze these concepts. Conrad names these structures—mathematical skills and problem solving skills—in both his course syllabus and the initial interview. The syllabus begins with a general statement about the important skills and understandings to be developed in Physics 1–2: "Physics 1–2 is a college preparatory course which will challenge your learning skills, enable you to apply your mathematical training, improve your word problem solving techniques, and introduce you to introductory topics of the vast realm of 'Physics.'" In this course, he teaches his students to apply their mathematical training, acquired elsewhere, to problems in dimensional analysis or unit analysis. He assumes a mastery of mathematical skills but deepens students' understanding of these skills by providing opportunities for their broader application. His syllabus spells out this assumption: "It is most strongly urged that you have completed Algebra 3-Trig prior to enrollment in this course. Without this background you will have a most difficult if not impossible task."

A more important analytical skill is the ability to solve word problems. In addition to mentioning improved "word problem solving techniques," Conrad's syllabus identifies the source of the problems and their solutions: "*Modern Physics* is the text used in this course. Virtually all of the problems you will work on and the explanatory materials necessary to solve these problems are contained in the text." In the initial interview, he further elaborates the process he uses to develop this skill. At the beginning of the school year, his students have the mathematical skills for physics but have limited ability to solve word problems. He spends time teaching problem solving strategies: reading the problem, drawing from the problem what it is that is to be solved, and gleaning information not only from the problem but from an understanding of concepts that have impact on the problem. He works hard to phrase questions in discussion and on tests to correspond to concepts emphasized in class. This, he notes, builds a student's confidence in problem solving and inspires closer checking of answers. Both unit analysis and problem solving assume the ability to read carefully and critically in order to translate words into a mathematical formula and then to solve it correctly.

Conrad's conception of the substance of physics is thus influenced by hierarchy and time. He has established an informal ranking of eighteen concepts composed of elemental relationships. He emphasizes two basic analytical skills to understand these concepts. Like the beginning teachers in the Baxter et al. study (1985), this view of simple relations among concepts may be related to Conrad's prior knowledge of physics; although he has a high level of training in biology, his preparation in physical science does not have the same breadth or depth. He thus sees simpler relationships within the field and focuses upon the wonder and surprise inherent in them.

PEDAGOGICAL KNOWLEDGE

In addition to knowledge of the nature of subject matter and knowledge of how one verifies and produces knowledge in a discipline, teacher knowledge also includes pedagogy, understanding of self, and understanding of students. This knowledge subsumes educational goals as well as beliefs about what good teaching is, pedagogical skills, notions about motivation, and knowledge of student's prior learning. Data from these four experienced teachers suggest that expert teachers select a controlling imagery from one component of teacher knowledge to represent this knowledge. While each teacher thinks about the landscape of content in profoundly different ways, each uses this image as a metaphorical bridge between teacher and student understandings of a discipline's cognitive structure and its analytical skills. Embedded in Bob's, Langdon's, Conrad's, and Linda's knowledge of subject matter and pedagogy, these images consequently shape the content that is understood by students.

The Game

For Bob, the centrality of power in historical events is "a game." This game imagery shapes the analogies selected for study. Students, for example, are asked to compare the American Revolutionary Army to "an untuned jalopy" or to "a collection of retired football players." Moreover, to show that he is also a game player, Bob accepts his students' suggested name of "Mr. Jellyblob" as the persona of a naive substitute. Further, Bob works to bring to students' awareness the emotions involved in any decision. "I have faith that values trigger learning," he says. "That's why I put an emphasis on the conflict in what we're studying or in the ways of doing something." He works toward an understanding of the human context for historical events. The purpose of the game is to challenge students to develop ideas more fully.

His understanding of student motivation and ability paces his game. To include in discussion as many students as possible, Bob begins his classes at the bell and frequently reviews concepts or principles discussed in the previous lesson. He explains in the initial interview:

I think setting the mood for each class to be involved is difficult because each class is different. In first period, the better students range from quiet to very verbal. The others . . . some are not good at listening because they are having a hard time understanding what is happening. If I were to keep them with me, I would take an enormous amount of my time, and I can't do that. But I don't feel comfortable about leaving them out, either.

He relies upon his clear organization and high expectations to secure for him student attention and involvement.

The contest is especially salient in his description of classroom discussion. Taking the offensive stance, Bob expects his game players to speak up and be counted. His students are to expect attacks and to respond defensively. This probing produces the game-like give and take of situations where the outcome is uncertain yet controlled ultimately by the success of the "players." He regularly emphasizes "the conflict in what we're studying or in the ways of doing something." Before students can agree that the primary motivation of a member of the Second Constitutional Convention was economic self-interest, they identify possible competing motivations. Bob probes responses and "attacks" student answers. "I ask them to give a defense of their answer and to have the courage to do so." For Bob, the perfect class session is "one where I feel uneasy that not all were listening but that most were. I feel energy and the kids do, too." It is an active, energetic hour. In this game imagery, Bob is a coach quite unlike Vince Lombardi: He notices each error but neither criticizes nor praises it until his students/players have sufficient confidence to accept correction.

The game imagery thus transforms Bob's conception that power is central to historical events into topics and interaction in reading, writing, and discussion. The game emphasizes alternative and opposing views, with its focus on conflict, strategies, and limits.

The Battle

Langdon expects students to be "aware of the debate in the battle for men's minds." This debate continues among people who want various kinds of societies and between advocates of democratic and authoritarian forms of government. Even the joy of learning, a goal that Langdon hopes to instill in students, is bought through hard work and conflict.

For Langdon, "the battle" of political ideologies is the heart of governance; this battle consists of opposing viewpoints contesting for the supremacy of one. Hence, there are political winners and losers. The debate imagery, evident in this inquiry into the nature of humankind and the nature of the state, transforms the teaching of content throughout Langdon's semester-long government course. In reviewing revolutionary communist theory, he reminds students about the need for an informed citizenry that understands opposing political views before attacking them. "It is clear from my reading of the law that it is necessary to learn the opponent's view—the difficulty we have with Marxists is that they know history better than those who believe in democracy." In distinguishing the nomination and election processes, he uses a battle metaphor: The nomination process is a "battle" to win delegates to the convention. Students are to select political principles they would "kill or die for." To imagine governmental institutions as a "ship of state" further develops the military imagery, focusing upon its enduring and competitive features.

Moreover, Langdon uses his organizing image of a debate or battle to secure student cooperation. His chief means of motivating students is to show interest in them as individuals in the classroom. His opening ritual each hour regularly includes verbal play with students. He is particularly pointed in teasing male students about wearing hats and sunglasses in the classroom: "Take the sunglasses off. I mean, you can leave those until you go to Hollywood. In the meantime, take off that lovely hat of yours." He also needles Arlis about tardiness and a scholarship award; he cautions Beth and Susan not to talk about their "unrequited loves"; and he suggests to Laura that "a girl could get fat" eating in the classroom. Although his raillery is delivered in a booming voice full of indignation, Langdon does not specify the consequences of this misbehavior; his purpose is to tease rather than to threaten students. Occasionally, he intends to motivate the entire group, as well as an individual, to continue hard work:

"You know, it just doesn't pay to give seniors a break. If I hear only one more parent ask me—'What do you think about this senior slump? My son or daughter talks about senior slump.'—I'm going to say, 'Mr. David's mother, . . . ' " [Mr. Selhorst had noticed that David was not listening and was pulling him back into the topic at hand. Dave's classmates giggled, anticipating the joking interchange that would follow.] " 'Such a thing is all a figment of your child's imagination designed and manufactured to explain away their incompetence, their indifference and their shoddy scholarship.' "

"You explained that to someone else's mother," Dave broke in, "because it wasn't my mother."

"Well, yes, it's a kind of network. It came up because I told someone else's mother, 'You know, one of the things you might do is have Suzi talk to her friends about her studies instead of just about her social life.' 'Well, she talks to David Larkin,' this mother said. And I said, 'Oh, god, what a waste of time! He's screwing around something terrible!' "

"But my mom doesn't know that," Dave protested.

"But those are the facts, aren't they?"

Langdon's students enjoy this teasing, especially when it is directed to someone else; the more self-confident students appreciate the exhibition of their social skills and, for them, the embarrassment of the teasing is worth the peer attention. Langdon does not tease the less self-confident; like an experienced debater, he selects his points and his targets carefully, in order to secure cooperation.

The battle imagery both shapes Langdon's choice of strategies and colors verbal exchanges in the classroom. Drawn from the heart of political activities, it permeates both the content and the climate of his classroom. Students are expected to stand and be counted.

The Journey

For Linda, literary analysis and composition are routes on a difficult "journey." The destination of literary travel is, fundamentally, an understanding of the text and, secondarily, a world of ideas from other disciplines that mediate an understanding of literature.

Like literature, this analytical journey travels from beginning to end and acknowledges both time and place; however, not all segments of the journey are easy. Linda encourages her students to view learning as a developmental process that holds intrinsic value for those who continue. In the initial interview, she expresses this goal as her wish to instill students with an appreciation for learning for its own sake, rather than for the grade or score it receives. Moreover, she encourages the delight in literary imagery and the enjoyment of sound in literature. But meaningful learning is not easy. Anticipating her students' difficulty in literary study, Linda ends her course syllabus with honest encouragement: "Some parts of this course may be tedious and even boring because they may require doing some of the mundane tasks that will eventually lead to the AP exam. Please stay with the work—put up with the tedium." Eventually, the careful attention to analysis and written expression will result in success on the AP exam: "You will be happy that you went through some of the painful and tedious exercises of the early part of the year." Eventually, Faulkner's long, complex sentences in *The Bear* will "sweep by" and their meaning become clear. Continuing the journey imagery, she adds, "What makes this book so marvelous, of course, is that once you get through it and figure out what it means, it's sort of like climbing Mt. Everest."

Because the goal of this journey is distant, Linda provides regular encouragement and occasional pleasure. Unlike Conrad and Langdon, who provide group experiences to motivate students, Linda coaches students individually. She spends far more time during the class session, especially at the beginning and the end of the hour, in talking with students about particular problems in their work. In part, this singular treatment is the result of her understanding about the nature of the group. Sixteen of the twenty-four students enrolled in her third-period class have been identified as gifted; of the remaining eight, she believes that two are gifted but have not been formally identified. This student characteristic makes the class unique in its ability to handle complex academic tasks. But this uniqueness brings other difficulties. Because these students have been grouped together since the first grade, they are sometimes cliquish and intolerant of differences. This causes both intragroup and intergroup difficulties. Andrea, for example, chooses to remain aloof from the group; she usually sits in the back corner of the room but does participate in discussion. Adrienne is also an isolate in this group; her New Wave preferences in dress and music attract frendships outside this class who are intolerable to her classmates. This group is unique in an additional way. Six students, one-fourth of the group, have learned English as their second rather than their primary language. This language background requires Linda to explain cultural interferences as well as content misunderstandings. Thus, at the bell each morning, Linda can be found surrounded by a group of students, each with an individual question.

On occasion, Linda provides coaching statements for the entire group. She begins her lesson on the Friday before spring vacation with the admonition to "look around the room and see all of the cowards" who are absent.

"Do you mean we could have turned in our Lear paper on Monday?" [Janis teased, knowing that the next Monday of school was more than a week away. Her classmates giggled].

"What I want to know," Rob began, "is do these people have over . . . do they still get credit? Well, I want to hear that?"

"It's a late paper," Ms. Reed replied. "It's a grade lower. And they must have been aware of that when they were weighing, yesterday, the consequences of their absence."

Linda replies with a story about her own experience in a similar situation and cautions students to recall that the absent ones will not devote an entire vacation week to their papers. Students who are present and diligent shared in this special time; they are urged to be tolerant of those who proceed at a different pace but are assured that just consequences follow all decisions.

Linda's image of an extended, difficult pilgrimage, drawn from her understanding of literary analysis and students, shapes her conception of the subject matter of literary study and her interactions with students. The end of these travels is college-level reading and writing. The means to that end is hard work, careful attention to detail, and challenging materials. Thus, the journey or pilgrimage presents a useful metaphor for communicating literary concepts and for explaining literary analysis.

The Magic

For Conrad, matter, energy, and light make reality a "magic land" of physical principles; these principles are sometimes counterintuitive and appear to require the suspension of established logic when unusual events occur. This wonderland is an unconventional world, peopled with anthropomorphic objects and images, rather like the animated world of children's television, which enlivens everyday reality. Further, this image makes learning interesting. Periodic interruptions in the class hour frequently take on the magical cast of advertisements for Physics-land.

Because he believes most students find high school boring and he is determined to make learning interesting, Conrad works to build a magical sense of community in his classroom. He spends time talking about rock concerts or other events that are important to his students. He also both teases and praises his students for outside activities. He knows something about each student: Ann is a peer counselor at the county mental health department, Daniel wears dark glasses because "it's cool," Juli has the "European look," Susan has just accepted UC Berkeley's offer of admission and rejected Stanford's, Chan refuses to tell him the good fishing spots on the bay, and Randy was just awarded a college scholarship. He has a keen sense of student ability and works to build confidence through praising those things that are going well and showing his care for students in a personal way.

Further, he shapes this caring into a cooperative effort: He will assist students in their college applications if they will help him, and he shares his life outside the classroom with them. Finally, he sponsors special classroom events that become part of the classroom mythology. Each year he selects a leitmotif that appears and reappears throughout his teaching. The theme this year, the Rocky Horror Picture Show, was most obviously apparent one April day when students came dressed as their favorite character from the show. Conrad is clear about this event and its purpose: It is designed to remotivate second-semester seniors for the last eight weeks of school.

During a unit on light, this magical imagery shapes the representation of dispersion and light mixing, and physical elements take on human characteristics. In Physics-land, frequencies are "chunked" instead of grouped or arranged. The optical spectrum is just a "pimple" on the face of the electromagnetic spectrum. If we are sensitive to the entire electromagnetic spectrum, the rays will "bombard our nervous system with a minor brainstorm." In color vision theory, light waves never stimulate retinal cones; they "tickle" them. To illustrate these principles, Conrad draws a color spectrum on the board with his "magic chalker"; he "throws" or "pops" filters into the lightbox, then "pumps" in the light. He highlights a demonstration of the color spectrum with this explanation:

And frequencies here... [with long sweeping arm motions, Mr. Rizzo pointed to ranges on the color spectrum]... tickle the blue cones; and frequencies here tickle the green cones; and frequencies here tickle the red cones. And when you see a white sheet of paper, all three kinds of your retinal cones are being tickled. And when you see something orange, more are being tickled in this region and fewer in this region to give you a shift to that region. And when you see black, none are being tickled!

Special magical characters inhabit this Physics-land. The primary colors are named "The Big Three." "Ghosts" live inside television sets. "The Stick Monster" turns shadows in the lightbox from blue to red to green. Blue light is "Berkeley blue"; the red filter is a "little guy" who "wouldn't let the blue through"; the blue filter "hides" from him but the cyan does not. The primary filters each "eat a share of the pie" of white light, and the lightbox produces all these "tricks." Conrad's clomping footsteps on the wooden demonstration platform represent "the Zombie" walking. "Happy Donuts" reward hard work, and perfection is "the essence of the Happy Donut." From a poster over the chalkboard, "Scotty, the Wonder-dog" demonstrates the center of gravity and the Second Law of Equilibrium; another poster promotes "worm love."

Finally, Physics-land has its own special language. The three components that constitute a Sony Trinitron are "trins." Wavelengths are "low freq, middle freq, and high freq—uencies" of light. "Narley" is an expression of wonder and surprise and a verb of motion: "So let's go narley over here." Colors become "el greeno" or "el whito." A "wowser" confirms a hypothesis. A "puppy" is something that one cares about, such as a television set or a color addition formula: it is also an expression of amazement, as in "son of a dead puppy!" Magic transforms everyday physical reality into something special.

The metaphor for Conrad's pedagogical thinking is drawn from a childlike view of physical reality. Like G. K. Chesterton's "logic of elfland" (1957), it represents inductive rather than deductive logic, a belief not commonly espoused among scientists. It is based more directly on Conrad's understanding of senioritis and of difficulties students have with physical concepts than on his understanding of current scientific practice.

SUMMARY

While each of the four teachers thinks about structure of content in profoundly different ways, each uses this structuring to shape and organize curricula. As such, their conceptions represent a solid foundation in subject matter. Bob places power at the center of historical study, encircled by social, economic, and political influences. Critical reading and effective writing and thinking are skills used to analyze these historical concepts. Langdon equates the concepts of governance, rights, and political views; he emphasizes clear writing, critical reading, and thinking. Linda identifies literary study as composed of textual analysis enhanced by ideas from other disciplines that mediate that understanding. Conrad conceives physics as a hierarchy of concepts headed by matter and energy; his primary conceptual skills are problem solving and unit analysis.

In addition to this subject matter knowledge, Bob, Langdon, Linda, and Conrad use knowledge of students and of self to transform these conceptions of subject matter as they prepare to represent them for students. Each selected a unique image—a game, a battle, a journey, and magic—to represent their knowledge. Although varying in the adequacy with which they represent content, these images view students as active agents in their own learning. For Bob, students are active players in the game of history. They must understand the social, political, and economic components of power. They use the skills of reading, writing, thinking, and oral presentation to develop these concepts. For Langdon, students are foot soldiers in political battles. To understand the structure, function, and process of government as causal and hierarchical, they must analyze ideology through writing, thinking, and critical reading skills. Linda and her students journey toward an understanding of concepts from sociology, philosophy, psychology, and aesthetics as they relate to particular literature. Her students use literary analysis and composition to interpret and convey the meaning of texts. For Conrad, students are skeptics at a magical show. Their understanding of the hierarchical structure of "matter" and "energy" must be demonstrated through the application of mathematical and problem solving skills.

Once these teachers have formulated this knowledge—the combination of subject matter and pedagogy, student motivation and personal goals— it is then presented to students in one of a number of different forms; and it is to the forms of representation that we now turn.

4

Transforming Content into Critical Thinking Tasks

Teaching critical thinking, based on a teacher's conception of content and shaped by pedagogical knowledge, is best understood through its presence in the classroom. In the act of instruction, this teacher knowledge takes on one of two manifestations. It is, first of all, understood by the narrative processes by which subject matter is represented for students. It is through a form of representation in explanation—ranging from the concrete or familiar to the more abstract and purely conceptual—that a teacher makes public this knowledge. Thus, when these teachers explain concepts to students, their narrative processes differ by their subject matter understanding, which in turn identifies concepts and cognitive processes required to access particular content, by the organizing image each has chosen to represent pedagogical knowledge, and by the forms of representation each has selected.

Second, this teacher knowledge shapes the academic tasks that are assigned to students. It is through the assignments they complete that students understand the nature of subject matter. Students interpret the work of history, government, literature, or physics by the work they produce in those classrooms. To understand how teachers teach reasoning, therefore, requires an investigation of both how subject matter understanding is represented to students and how that understanding is transformed into work tasks for students. Meaningful thought is developed through students' actions that represent transformations of a teacher's particular subject matter understanding.

Further, the effectiveness of these forms of representation and academic tasks is based upon the extent to which the organizing imagery is appropriate and beneficial to students. Based upon comparison, metaphors can represent pedagogical content knowledge in particularly striking ways. They do render the incomprehensible more accessible and, as such, they are useful vehicles for instruction; but their boundaries are often uncertain and open to misinterpretation. For example, if a metaphor to represent pedagogy is misinterpreted by students to represent content as well as pedagogy, content misunderstandings may occur.

FORMS OF REPRESENTATION

In Bob's, Langdon's, Linda's, and Conrad's classrooms, pedagogical content knowledge is represented in narrative processes and explanations for students. In this transformation, subject matter concepts that are linguistic, visual, auditory, numerical, or tactile take shape in words, drawings, sounds, numbers, or experiences. Since what is learned is a function of both content and method, multiple forms teach wider conceptions of reality. Bob, Langdon, Linda, and Conrad choose to represent their subject matter through a variety of representations. All four teachers rely heavily upon linguistic forms, particularly the conventional linguistic form of text materials. All four use voice as vehicles of thought; three use visual forms to communicate concepts; and two use numerical abstractions to show relationships. The differences in their conceptions of content structure and their pedagogical imagery, however, result in different narrative processes and uses of these forms.

The Game

Bob illustrates the offensive and defensive moves of historical "games" through extensive use of visual imagery. His drawings map the game plans for the political spectrum, for the motivations for political action, and for the short-term and long-term reactions to the Stamp Act. Compared to the other three teachers, Bob's images convey more elaborate concepts and require more student participation. His most complex mimetic device is a diagram for an extended definition of the Stamp Act, a visual image that extracts the salient features of the Colonists' reactions and represents them as a game plan (Figure 4–1).

This graphic outline is designed to show the relationship between components of the Stamp Act and its effects. It also indicates to students the complexity of detail necessary to analyze this concept. Bob completes half of the analysis and leaves the remainder for students. The following day, he structures a much simpler form to conclude a discussion of the motivations to political action (Figure 4–2). Students use this diagram to summarize which principles under discussion—freedom, moral values, place or status, or power—would stimulate interest in political change and which would support the status quo. These drawings are reminiscent of diagrams

Figure 4–1
Diagram of an Analysis of an Extended Definition of an Historical Event

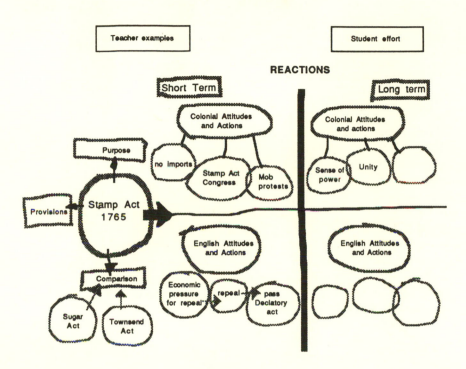

Figure 4–2
Diagram of Forces of Change in an Historical Event

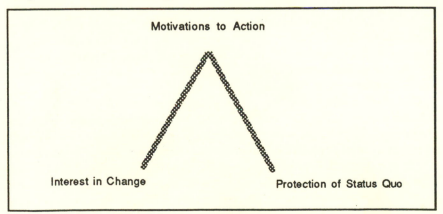

Figure 4–3
Diagram for Developing Arguments Relating to a Concept

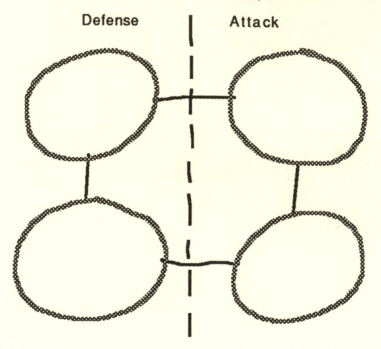

"Jeremiah Wynkoop is a spineless jellyfish who becomes a revolutionary only because the ties of conflict push him to the beach of no return."

Defend and attack this statement with evidence placed in the four circles below

Defense   Attack

drawn by color commentators during televised football games or basketball coaches during time-out.

Similar visual images on written assignments help students organize data in support of a point of view. To prepare for a writing assignment, Bob gives students a biased statement about Jeremiah Wynkoop, a fictional historical figure, which they were both to defend and to attack by citing specific evidence from their reading (Figure 4–3). The placement of the circles and their interconnections suggest that supporting evidence for each side is to be composed of two independent but equal statements connected by a uniform perspective on Wynkoop. On another occasion, Bob expands this comparison to include both personal qualities and political attitudes and values.

In addition to visual representation, Bob uses metaphor to provide mimesis in narrative structures. In metaphoric comparisons to games and sports, students think about historical concepts in a new way. When discussing the political spectrum, for example, Bob asks students to "name the part of an automobile which locates the essence of liberalism, moderation, and conservatism." The next day, he expands this metaphor in an assignment he names "Brain Fertilizer #1," a preparation for discussion:

The wise old man was long troubled with how best to use his jar of *moderate essence* in his new car. He considered and rejected the following possibilities: windshield wipers, backseat, muffler, steering wheel, headlights, and ignition. Briefly hypothesize why the old man might have considered each item as a possibility and why he ultimately rejected each item.

By asking students to explain why each part was considered and why it was rejected, Bob reminds students of alternative perspectives in all historical events. On another occasion, to prepare students for a discussion on the Revolutionary War, Bob offered two metaphors. Students were then to select the one description most insightful and valid and to list characteristics of the army suggested by that image: "The American Revolutionary Army was an untuned jalopy driven by Superman without gas or a road map in a race with BMWs and Jaguars"; and "The American Revolutionary Army was a collection of retired football players volunteering to help Joe Montana win the Super Bowl." Although these mimetic vehicles are open to varied interpretation, they consistently represent concepts in powerful verbal images and suggest the game playing in historical decision.

Supporting this mimesis is a more conventional explanation in the form of textbook and reminders. For a unit on the revolutionary period, for example, Bob assigns "America Secedes from the Empire," Chapter 6 of *American Pageant* and a reading on Sam Adams from *Politics in Massachusetts*. He also assigns an extensive review of the textbook chapter, consisting of true-false, multiple-choice, and short-answer questions. Occasionally, even conventional discourse contains imaginative or representational references to the game or to training routines. Bob's assignments attend to spacing and format, as Conrad's do, but add line and illustration. On the Friday before spring vacation, for example, he reminds students of their vacation assignments (Figure 4–4).

Bob also explains historical concepts through expressive works, used both as texts for student interpretation and as tasks requiring reasoning skills. They read Arthur Miller's *The Crucible* in order to understand colonial social history. They read "The Spirit of '76" by Carl Becker, a fictionalized imperfect manuscript about Jeremiah Wynkoop, an eighteenth-century lawyer

Figure 4-4
Chalkboard Reminder for Vacation Assignments

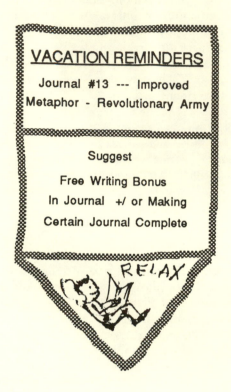

from New York. This reading became the basis for a letter-writing assignment, in which students were to write to Josiah Quincy about having met Jeremiah at the Second Continental Congress. Their assignment read: "In your letter you are reflective, striving to create an accurate and vivid description of how two people could share so much and yet view the world so differently. In your letter, you also are intent on persuading Josiah that your radical perspective is what these times have needed." Bob adds this admonition: "Unlike today, letter writing in the eighteenth century was a real art. We want you to become part of the tradition." Students are to understand the social values of eighteenth-century life as well as its political postures.

Bob's use of simulations also narrates both factual and emotional aspects of an historical event. In the first half of the spring term, his students reenact the Boston Tea Party and the Continental Congress. There they assume the roles of actual participants, study the position taken by a participant in the conflict, and represent that position in re-creating the event. They imitate conversation and conflicts of the actual event and they convey the essence of the event in their own words. The simulation shares some structural similarity to the original; although highly schematized and condensed in time, it provides students with an understanding of what the event meant to those who participated in it along with its provisions and consequences.

Bob explains historical content through structures that permit him to develop the game analogy. The story of history is carried through textbook readings. Historical values and perspectives are conveyed through literature, drawings, simulations, and letter writing. He is aware of the limitations of these analogies. He explains in an interview: "I've also decided there is value in bad analogies. I used to spend hours searching for the perfect analogy and then it wouldn't work. Now I use all kinds, like 'How is George Washington like a watermelon?' If it's awful, students can criticize it." These narrative processes are consistent with his game plan and pedagogical content knowledge.

The Battle

In Langdon's classroom, the battle image provides a screen in selecting forms for narrating content. To convey these battles, most of his forms of representation permit mapping of strategies or illustrate conquered and unconquered territory. Mimetic visual forms, for example, organize information into opposing categories. One handout, designed to accompany a unit discussion of the political spectrum, compares democratic and authoritarian forms of government; these hemispheres are further subdivided into a liberal and a conservative quadrant or a radical and a reactionary quadrant (Figure 4–5). All forms of government are assumed to fit into one of the quadrants; further, all political systems can be identified as either democratic or authoritarian.

To show the forces upon political decisions, Langdon uses the map. To explain the Marxist theory of history, he refers to a large pull-down map of Europe that hangs at the front of his classroom. Using the Roman Empire to illustrate dialectic progression, he points to the expanding and shrinking boundaries that result from these shaping forces.

Explanations take on a debate coloration as Langdon emphasizes key ideas through repetition. Here, interactions with students become an exercise in turn-taking. For example, when reviewing the tasks of a nominating convention, he repeats each purpose before identifying the next:

"Ok, that's one thing—they have to agree on the party platform. What's the second thing they have to do?"
"Nominating," Ted said.
"They have to nominate."

Figure 4–5
One Diagram of a Political Spectrum

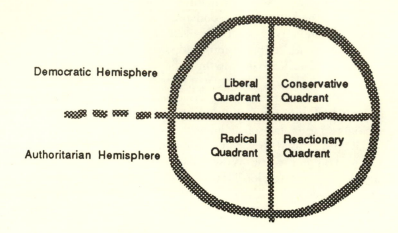

"Vice President and President," Greg spoke up.

"President and Vice President. Ok, those things are obvious. What's the third thing they have to do?"

To direct student attention to different aspects of the political spectrum, Langdon uses both conventional and expressive forms of narrative and explanation. He assigns an article on "Socialism and Karl Marx" from *The Age of the Economist*. He provides direct statements of assumptions and assignments. The first page of his Unit 3 handout, for example, outlines the four written assignments, the exam question, and the important assumptions underlying "The Political Spectrum in Theory and Practice." His assignments ask students to develop a position: "Explain the differences between the Democrats and Republicans, and explain the role of third parties in the American political system. State how you would register to vote today, if you were eligible, and explain your reasons." To present a third political view, Langdon assigns "The Grand Inquisitor" from Dostoyevsky's *The Brothers Karamazov*. Students are asked to defend or attack the Inquisitor's view of human nature and the good state.

Finally, Langdon explains concepts through the use of specialized abbreviations and codes in his boardwork. For example, in discussing the political view of revolutionary communism, he summarizes its three prophesies in a central list:

Prophesies
1. WWR
2. D of P
3. WA of S

Figure 4–6
Representation of a Marxist View of Social Structure

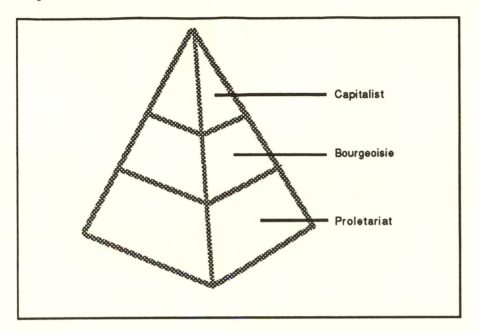

These symbolize "world wide revolution" (WWR), "dictatorship of the proletariat" (D of P), and "withering away of the state" (WA of S). Similarly, he illustrates dialectical progression and historical evolution through thesis and antithesis with Ts, As, and arrows. On another occasion, explaining the point count for a unit test on the political spectrum, he selects special abbreviations for specific concepts in the political spectrum: "Political Spectrum," in fact, becomes "PS," the "Grand Inquisitor" becomes "GI."

Langdon maps parlimentary democracy, the nomination process, dialectic progression, a time-line of the two party system, the Marxist interpretation of capitalist society, and the coalitions in the Republican and Democratic parties in symbolic visual forms. To represent a Marxist interpretation of capitalist society, he chooses a pyramid (Figure 4–6). He explains the distinctions between those who own the wealth, the capitalists, and those who manage and serve the capitalists, the bourgeoisie. To prevent his students from contemporary bourgeoisie aspirations, Langdon narrates a nineteenth-century social context. He reminds students of the abuses brought by industrialization: child labor, limited schooling, poor working conditions, and the docility of the workers, particularly women.

Four days later he illustrates the differences between the nomination process and the election process (Figure 4–7). The delegates to the nominating convention, selected either through primaries or caucuses, elect a party

Figure 4–7
Chart Illustrating Differences Between Presidential Nomination and Election Processes

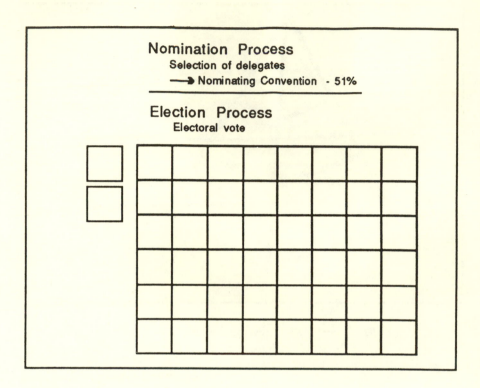

nominee with 51 percent of the vote. The election process begins on the first Tuesday following the first Monday in November, when voters of each state, represented by the grid, select electors to the Electoral College. The number of electors is dependent upon the size of the state's congressional delegation. The visual imagery suggests the differences in these two processes: Election is at once the more complex and more uniform of the two.

On another occasion, numerical abstractions chart the arithmetic combinations of factions in a party coalition. Earlier Langdon had charted a timeline to show the chronological development of the American two-party system. This time, a more abstract drawing borrows the symbolic use of letters and subscripts from mathematics to illustrate the infinite number of combinations of factions that may occur in any one party (Figure 4–8). In the discussion that accompanies this image, Langdon names the groups that have historically made up the Republican and Democratic parties. He uses the abstraction, however, to map the current transitional period in each party; neither party's coalitions are firmly held together. Thus, visual im-

Figure 4–8
Mathematical Model for Political Parties

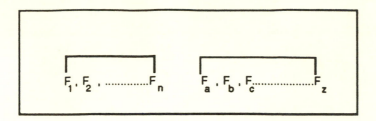

agery represents the essence of each position and reduces the argument to its central tenets.

Langdon's explanation of political concepts draws heavily upon his battle imagery. Narrative processes illustrate direct opposition of political views through maps and illustrations, through direct statement, and through specialized codes. But while these specialized codes are appropriate to military strategics and covert operations, they may have the effect of mystifying rather than encapsulating ideas, rendering students outsiders rather than participants. They may be metaphorically appropriate but pedagogically unsound.

The Journey

Linda's literary pilgrimage is founded in the text but may range widely from there. Her explanations are usually short, more like a descriptive itinerary than detailed narrations: The specifics are provided en route. In the fall semester, students read Henry James's *The American*, Dostoyevsky's *Crime and Punishment*, and Camus's *The Plague* and *The Stranger*; in the spring their journey includes poetry, Shakespeare's *King Lear*, and Faulkner's *The Bear*.

To train students in the kinds of thinking necessary to complete this journey, she assigns selected critical essays from *20th Century Culture* and *Introductory Readings in Literary Criticism*. These essays explain by modeling appropriate critical thinking. To explain the importance of attention to detail, Linda develops short statements summarizing important points for distribution to students. Most of these are declarative statements, which have the effect of safety reminders, as in this summary of punctuation rules:

The comma is used to set off

A. *Independent Clauses* when they are joined by coordinate conjunctions (and, but, or, nor, for): He is fond of fishing, but she prefers hiking.

A page of essay review questions for the Lear paper narrates more detailed information about the itinerary: "In some novels and plays certain parallel or recurring events prove to be significant. In an essay, describe the major similarities and differences in a sequence of parallel or recurring events in a novel or play and discuss the significance of such events." Occasionally, these narrative statements are in the form of questions rather than explanation, as in the reading guide for *The Bear*: "2) What is the significance of the various ages of Ike in the story? Why is it important that he was 10 when he first came to the woods ('two ciphers')? What are the other key ages?"

Occasionally, Linda posts travel reminders in an abbreviated agenda or a list of principles to remember. She outlines on the chalkboard the two activities to be accomplished in one class experience:

1. proofreading
2. *The Bear*

During a discussion of Lear, she records qualities identified in major characters. This board notation took the form of a list. Gloucester shows "less pride; a lack of understanding; foolish, mercurical actions; and an unwillingness to accept responsibility." Kent is "loyal, proactive, intelligent, assertive, and honest." These conventional visual forms are more like signposts on a trail than an attempt to make full meaning public.

Linda explains literary concepts through narrative processes that corroborate her journey imagery. Literary concepts are applied in analyses of texts; composing concepts are developed as analyses are communicated. Hers is largely a written and oral journey; although visual forms are appropriate to a travel metaphor—in the form of maps, for example—Linda does not draw upon graphic representation in understanding and analyzing literature.

The Magic

The magic in Conrad's pedagogical content knowledge is drawn primarily from his understanding of student motivation; therefore, imaginative interactions color his narration, but content is presented in more traditional ways than his imagery would suggest. He relies upon one central text, *Modern Physics*, to provide the reading, problem sets, and labs for his course. Students read a chapter on reflection, then one on refraction, then one on diffraction and polarization. They complete the prepared accompanying labs on concave mirrors, on the index of refraction of glass, on converging lenses, and on the focal length of a lens. The chapter test on refraction includes direct statements and unambiguous questions: "(4) A 2 cm object is placed 7 cm in front of a converging lens. The lens has a focal length of

5 cm. How far from the lens is the image formed? (5) What is the size of the image in problem 4?"

In order to communicate clearly, Conrad attends to lines, spacing, and format as well as to words to explain concepts. In one corner of the board, he lists the daily activities for his biology and physics classes:

Bio Test
    Monday
Physics
    Thought Problems
    Problem Set
    Pass Out Labs

Like his conception of physics, these lists are hierarchical and conventional and are traditional explanations. On another occasion, during a discussion of refraction, he develops a master list of formulas for mixing light:

$$R + B + G \rightarrow \text{white}$$
$$B + G \rightarrow \text{cyan}$$
$$R + G \rightarrow \text{yellow}$$
$$R + B \rightarrow \text{magenta}$$

In these formulas, "R" stands for "red," "B" for "blue," and "G" for "green." Combinations of two or three colors are added to produce light. But each formula, in addition to showing the additive properties of light, also indicates subtractive features: The empty space indicates the color that when subtracted from white will produce the same result.

To communicate his explanations, Conrad regularly uses chalkboard drawings to represent concepts. Here, he presents illustrations of a principle or graphic representations of the relations among concepts. These forms include the relationship between an image and a convex lens, the electromagnetic spectrum, the pathway of light through a prism, and the refraction of light traveling from water to air. Each of these drawings is simplified to focus upon the key elements of the concept; many were selected from text drawings but were repeated in a new context. For example, Conrad drew the electromagnetic spectrum to explain the small but important optical spectrum (Figure 4–9).

In his discussion, Conrad identifies the infrared and ultraviolet rays but does not include them in order to keep the illustration simple. Before calculating the lambdas, he asks students why they should be satisfied with a sensitivity to only a small part of this spectrum. Later in the same lesson, he drew the path of light through a prism to illustrate that the placement of color is determined by the angle of refraction (Figure 4–10).

He recounts a conversation with a student before school; they had spec-

Figure 4–9
Visual Field of the Electromagnetic Spectrum

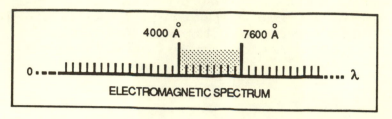

Figure 4–10
Diagram of Dispersion of Light

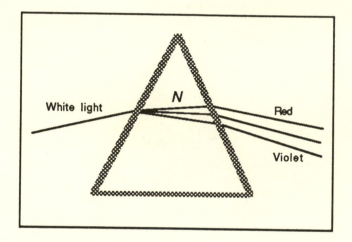

ulated on the relative positions of red and blue, then had completed a few
angle computations to verify each position:

We found out that red is refracted—if 30 degrees comes in, it will be refracted at
19.3. And the blue is refracted at 19.1, or whatever. Mathematically, this is what
is happening. The prism has a variety of N's. . . . So the separation is based upon
the physics principle that this chapter is titled after—*Refraction.*

In demonstrations and lab sessions, Conrad's visual forms are not drawings but objects or scientific equipment that represent various physical principles. He uses a model of an eyeball to show the lens properties of the
cornea. He uses a mercury vapor lamp to demonstrate the relationship
between heat and color. To demonstrate that color is a property of light,
he asks students to identify red and green papers while he floods the room
with red light. He uses a lightbox and filters to show how colors are added

by transmission of light. Each object or piece of equipment represents a physical principle with real world application; they illustrate his narration by focusing upon the essence of each principle.

In addition to drawings and models, numerical forms of representation appear regularly in Conrad's explanations of physical concepts. Most frequently, his concepts are represented by formulas. The numerical representation of object-image relationships, for example, is presented in this formula:

$$\frac{h_i}{h_o} = \frac{s_i}{s_o}$$

That is, the ratio of object size (h_i) to image size (h_o) equals the ratio of the object distance (s_i) to image distance (s_o). Similarly, light can be added or subtracted like numbers:

$$B \ + \ G \ = \ cyan$$
$$W \ - \ R \ = \ cyan$$

The addition of two primary colors produces cyan, the complement to red; the subtraction of red from white is also cyan.

Conrad's explanation of physical principles is not colored by his magical imagery but instead is conveyed by more conventional narrative processes. The major explanation is found in the text. Demonstrations, models, and figures supplement and illustrate this explanation. Unlike in the other teachers' pedagogical content knowledge, magical imagery connects but does not integrate Conrad's pedagogical content knowledge. It remains peripheral to the forms selected for representing content, the central vehicle for communicating physics to students.

ACADEMIC TASKS

While narrative processes, which convey a teacher's pedagogical content knowledge, explain higher order thinking processes, they do not reveal the kinds of thinking students are required to perform. These are contained in the academic tasks assigned to students. Consonant with their concepts of content, the four teachers in this study devoted the majority of classroom time to developing reasoning through academic tasks. When Bob, Langdon, Linda, and Conrad talk about the activities in their classrooms, they focus upon those tasks requiring the higher order cognitive skills necessary to understanding. These are work assignments in which "some information about the character of the correct answer [is] withheld so that memory cannot be used to accomplish the task. In addition, understanding tasks are often not easily reduced to a predictable algorithm" (Doyle, 1983, pp. 183–184). In tasks requiring reasoning, students have a clear definition of the product to be produced—for example, an analysis of the poem, "Poetry of Departures," in an AP writing—but the number of literary devices to use and the organization of ideas cannot be figured into a precise formula. All four teachers use their pedagogical content knowledge to guide the selection of a finite number of tasks to develop reasoning skills; this knowledge also shapes each task's precise nature. Even when declared important, unless an activity figures in the grade calculation, it does not directly communicate an interpretation of content.

The Game

For Bob, the game emphasizes a focus upon the group, or representatives of a group, rather than upon individual actors. Idiosyncratic personalities and singular psychological motivations are of lesser importance. Instead, the focus on opposing groups and teamwork stresses task strategies calling upon comparison and contrast. But there is also a playful quality to "the game"; one can experiment with strategies and take greater risks because the game's outcome is not a life-or-death matter. Thus, both this oppositional nature of groups and its playfulness shape the reasoning tasks in Bob's classroom.

The advocacy and opposition of a game dominate Bob's essay assignments. Once in each three to four-week unit, students develop a persuasive or comparative essay. For example, they were to assume the voice of Sam Adams and, in a letter to Josiah Quincy, comment upon a particular, imaginary event at the Second Continental Congress.

You are Sam Adams attending the Second Continental Congress in Philadelphia where you meet Jeremiah Wynkoop. During the Congress, you have come to know Jeremiah very well because you have talked for hours about the events leading up to the reality of revolution. Although you have come to respect Jeremiah for his strong integrity, you remain outraged at his general approach to political life. One night, you sit down and write a letter to Josiah Quincy back in Boston in which you try to compare your life, and particularly your political values and actions, with the life, values, and actions of Jeremiah.

This highly complex task requires, first of all, that students understand the game of political decision making. To complete the task, they must define the life, political values, and actions of Adams and Wynkoop; then they need to identify Adams' views of Wynkoop, to imagine how Adams would describe Wynkoop to a friend; finally, they must shape these ideas into eighteenth-century letter writing style. In addition to assigned texts, Bob suggests students might read background books about the Revolutionary era in general or on the role of radicals and Sam Adams in particular and about writing comparative essays.

Students are accountable for a well-supported comparison; they are further encouraged to add an instinctive flair to the expression of these ideas. Bob adds a postscript to this assignment: "The key to an acceptable paper is thoughtful comparison that is clearly written. If you can get into the role of Sam Adams and sense his thoughts and feelings, however, the letter may come more alive for you and make the assignment more interesting and fun." A section from Robin's letter indicates the extent to which Bob's students were able to accomplish this task.

Although I never thought I could possibly spend more than two minutes with a man with such timid, lukewarm ideas, I found myself in the company of Mr. Wynkoop for hours on end. I discovered that even though we are vastly different, there are a few important similarities between us in which you would be interested.

Firstly, just as I hold my religion as one of the most important aspects of my life, Mr. Wynkoop is also very religious and has tremendous moral character. I really admire the almost philosophical way he goes about his busy life. Also, Mr. Wynkoop attended the prestigious Kings College. It was very exhilarating to talk with such an intellectual man.

A unit essay topic on the Revolutionary Era requires similar cognitive skills in comparison:

Rossiter and Jensen viewed the American Revolution in sharply contrasting ways. Illustrate their differences in approach by looking at the meaning and importance of the Declaration of Independence and one other event. Conclude your essay with a brief statement in support of the position you find most convincing.

The response to this topic requires students to identify Rossiter's and Jensen's views on the importance of the Declaration of Independence, select one other historical event about which they also share conflicting views and explain the views of each, then interpret one view as the more compelling. Both of these written assignments ask students to take an advocacy position for one side in a historical power game.

Even extended definitions of historical events require comparisons. For these assignments, students are given, in advance, copies of the two questions from which the exam will be taken and the precise formula for generating the written response. For the unit "The Spirit of '76," students were required to provide an extended definition for either the Stamp Act or the Boston Tea Party. Their 250-word definition must incorporate these guidelines:

1. Place your event in time.
2. Describe the causation of the event.
3. Describe both the immediate and long range impact.
4. Contrast the event with related events to highlight its uniqueness.
5. Describe key roles played by specific individuals or groups.
6. Describe the event from more than one perspective.

The task requires students both to understand basic information about each event and its participants and to apply this information flexibly in interpreting its impact and in presenting it from multiple perspectives. Students are able to prepare an individual response for each definition before the test and memorize it; the actual writing may be a routine task, but the preparation promotes critical thinking.

Written tasks that develop memory or routine require the reproduction of information from previous presentation, either in class or in textual materials. In Bob's classroom, a written task requiring memory or routine is that portion of chapter tests containing objective questions. These generally are expressed as identification or multiple choice items.

12._____ The autocratic Catholic power that provided America with half of her regular armed forces and practically all of her naval strength.
13._____ An able American general known as the "Fighting Quaker."
14._____ This bold frontiersman led an expedition down the Ohio River to take three British forts in the Illinois country by surprise (Bailey and Kennedy, 1983, p. 33).

Here, the task asks students to read the question carefully, to recall the names of individuals and groups from the Revolutionary era, and to match the names with the statement. They are accountable for the correct identification and for correct spelling or a close approximation.

A majority of the academic tasks in Bob's classroom require higher order thinking skills. Major tasks such as the Sam Adams letter or an extended definition of an historical event require the marshalling, analysis, organization, and presentation of a large amount of information. His students are expected to state their positions in the game of history.

The Battle

For Langdon, governing reifies an ongoing debate. Like the image of the game, this image focuses upon the group, or representatives of a group, rather than upon individuals. Like the game, this image highlights the contrast between groups and calls for frequent comparisons. Unlike the game, however, the battle is a more serious, calculated, and compelling image. Battles are not playful or lighthearted occurrences but are called into being only after serious threat to life or property. The serious weight of this image guides the transformation of Langdon's pedagogical content knowledge into work tasks for students.

The battle is most pronounced in tasks that challenge assumptions about democratic and authoritarian forms of government and that require an understanding of opposing political views. For the unit on "The Political Spectrum in Theory and Practice," the essay exam question asked students to

describe in detail the way the political values of man work in theory and practice. Distinguish the specific differences between Left and Right and between the democratic and non-democratic hemispheres. Apply the above principles to the American two party system as it relates to Democrats, Republicans, and to third parties.

This task requires students to discuss the application of political values to theory and to the American two-party system through the use of specific example. Resources are "The Grand Inquisitor" chapter of *The Brothers Karamazov*, Marx's "Communist Manifesto," notes from class discussions and presentations, the unit outline, and their weekly written assignments.

Short written assignments also ask students to defend or oppose a particular political philosophy. For example, one weekly assignment from the unit "The Political Spectrum in Theory and Practice" states: "Read the 'Communist Manifesto' by Karl Marx or some other source and explain Marx's view of the nature of man and of the good society. After you have explored his reasoning in detail, state whether you agree or disagree with his philosophy and why." The task requires students, first, to analyze the question; second, to identify the resources of information for solving the problem—here the "Manifesto" or a similar source; third, to describe Marxian philosophy of human nature; and, finally, to assemble and state those ideas with clarity. Both these written tasks are designed to develop independent political thought through confronting ideas in a meaningful way.

Academic tasks in Langdon's classroom consist of knowing at least two sides of an issue and stating a position in the debate. These critical thinking tasks are serious, straightforward, and highly reasoned.

The Journey

Linda's journey is a more intimate, personal image than the battle or the game. One's success on a journey is linked to interpersonal relationships among the travelers, like Chaucer's Canterbury pilgrims, as well as to individual effort. In addition, a journey conveys psychological growth developed through confronting the unfamiliar and through mastering necessary skills. Thus, the academic tasks in Linda's classroom require more attention to psychological issues of individuals than groups and stress development of the cognitive processes of reading and writing.

Linda's literary journey is segmented by culminating essays that develop particular skills in analyzing literary texts and in organizing ideas; like a journey, the skills are organized sequentially, from simple to complex, each segment requiring increasing amounts of independence. In the fall and winter, for example, Linda suggests possible essay topics that students select and transform into an original thesis. By April, students devise original topics and theses themselves. An approved thesis then determines the organization and length of each paper.

To assist students in this independent thinking, Linda requires that each essay be developed in portions and checked before continuing; for their Lear paper, ten days before the essays are due, students submit their proposed theses for approval. Within that week, Linda meets with each of her twenty-four third-period students to suggest revisions. Her general statement reminds students about the value of this essay and the criteria for accountability: "My principal criteria for grading the content of the essay are logic, sequence, and sufficiency of development of the thesis." Nonetheless, students are also accountable for mechanical errors: "Make your assertions clear and effectively worded. You will lose one point for each different error."

Just as successful journeys require attention to detail, some of Linda's academic tasks demand critical reading and skillful writing. The AP writing assignments ask students to analyze a literary selection in a limited period of time. Here, the topic for the writing is identified and the literature, although not previously studied, is brief. But the student still must decide upon the praticular ideas to receive emphasis and organization. One question asks students to "read the following poem carefully and then write an essay in which you discuss how the poet's diction (choice of words) reveals his attitude toward the two ways of living mentioned in the poem." This task, while it is more precise than the essay assignment, is also more restricted in time. It requires students to indentify the two ways of living discussed in the poem, to indentify the poet's attitude toward them, and to support that assertion with evidence form poetic diction; it also requires a student to produce an answer in thirty minutes. As resources, students refer to the text and to their knowledge of poetry, diction, and literary analysis.

For a quiz on Acts IV and V of King Lear (Shakespeare/Kittredge, 1940), students are asked to explain quotations by identifying the speaker, the audience, the situation, and the significance of each. Some passages are brief: "I killed the slave that was a-hanging thee" (V, iii, 274). Others are longer:

        Was this a face
To be opposed against the warring winds?
To stand against the deep dread-bolted thunder?

In the most terrible and nimble stroke
Of quick, cross lightning? (IV, vii, 31–35).

Students are not expected to have memorized these passages; but they are expected to have read the two acts carefully and to be able to apply the meaning of these lines to character and events. Later, this information serves as resource ideas for the Lear essay.

Linda's academic tasks are developed in segments, like a journey. The reasoning that results in a critical essay is developed through attention to the details of literature as well as to its significance.

The Magic

For Conrad, concepts from physics, in themselves, are abstract and impersonal, but human interpretation makes them magical. Their counter-intuitive nature contributes to the mystery: For example, ice has more volume than steam, and color resides in light rather than pigment. One can use these principles like a magician uses illusion, as entertainment. Since Conrad's imagery is more emphasized in the presentation of assignments than in the nature of the work task itself, it provides a human aura to these abstract principles.

True to magic's peripheral nature, the academic tasks in this classroom are straightforward in nature. Conrad works to phrase questions on tests so that answers correspond to concepts emphasized in class. This builds student confidence in problem solving—they recognize the logic of the answer—and inspires closer checking of answers. The task involved in solving these problems requires reading the problem carefully, identifying what is to be solved, applying information from an understanding of physical concepts to establish the formula, and completing the calculations. Conrad's course syllabus outlines the purpose of tests and student accountability.

Tests are problem solving tests. Problem answer is to be placed in a box; scientific notation and units must be included. Actual work and set of the problem including key formulas used are to be placed in the workspace.

The point value of the test will vary with the number of problems (generally 50 points per test).

His commentary is straightforward and direct.

A second reasoning task, labs and their reports, permits students to perform some wizardry themselves. The unit on Refraction, for example, contained labs on concave mirrors, the index of refraction of glass, converging lenses, and focal lengths. In each, the task is to predict outcome, then to follow a scientific procedure, to record observations at various stages in this procedure, to perform calculations with the data generated in the observations, and to interpret this information. Occasionally, interpretive questions also require the flexible application of this knowledge. For example, the lab on converging lenses included these questions: "Why is it better to use the sun as the distant object than it is to use a house or tree when finding the focal length of the lens?" and "Give a practical application of each of the six cases of image formation by convex lenses." Students are accountable for completing almost all of the labs if they wish laboratory science credit for university admission.

Conrad's students are expected to show their reasoning on unit tests and lab reports. These academic tasks do require the use of higher order thinking processes; however, like Conrad's narrative processes, they are relatively uninfluenced by his magical imagery.

SUMMARY

The narrative processes and academic tasks that teachers devise for students make public the teachers' content knowledge and transform this understanding into student performance. An organizing imagery drawn from one aspect of a teacher's background knowledge shapes the representation of content and the selection of academic tasks and activities for students.

In this study, four experienced secondary teachers use explanation to unfold their subject matter knowledge and pedagogical thinking. These narrative structures take on a variety of forms of representation—verbal, visual, oral, numerical, or experiential—and are treated conventionally, mimetically, or expressively. These structures explain higher order thinking processes necessary for study in a particular discipline.

Explanations communicate teachers' content knowledge. But the critical thinking students are expected to perform is contained in academic tasks assigned to students. Consonant with their deep understanding of content, Bob, Langdon, Linda, and Conrad also devote the most time to academic tasks that require higher order processing skills. Thus, in Bob's classroom, the game imagery colors written and discussion tasks, requiring students to compare an event's impact on competing groups or to contrast economic theory to sport machinery. In Langdon's government classroom, the battle imagery focuses student attention on contrasting political alliances in writing and discussion. In Linda's English classroom, the journey imagery emphasizes issues inherent in course materials; literary journeys consist of periods of careful attention to detail—that is, periods of reading and discussion—interspersed by milestones, the unit essays. For Conrad, the controlling image of magic more directly informs the presentation of information than the selection of classroom activities and academic tasks; it nonetheless represents a pervasive human quality in abstract physical principles. His students interpret word problems and generate and confirm hypotheses through problem sets, lab reports, and discussion. Despite the pressures chronicled in recent studies of secondary teaching (Applebee, 1981; Boyer, 1983; Goodlad, 1983; Mitman, Mergendoller, Packer, and Marchman, 1984) Bob, Langdon, Linda, and Conrad were able to translate their conceptions of content primarily into critical thinking tasks and to support the completion of these tasks with other classroom activities.

Since learning is the result of negotiated interactions between teachers and students, an understanding of how content is transformed into critical thinking tasks is not sufficient. While a teacher's pedagogical transformation of content establishes the intended cognitive goal, the kind of cognitive skills all students use is determined by observing students work through a task rather than by studying the assignment or its product. Whether a critical thinking task accomplishes its designated purpose, then, and develops reasoning skills, depends upon both its design and its management in the classroom.

5

Managing Critical Thinking Tasks

Within the classroom, certain activities (usually presentations) involve the representation of teachers' understanding of subject matter through explanation. Certain other activities (usually written assignments) contain tasks that require the use of students' thinking skills. In the classrooms of Bob, Langdon, Linda, and Conrad, the use of the higher order thinking skills predominate in these critical thinking tasks. Their instruction and interactions regarding these academic tasks are consonant with the accountability system: The tasks are carefully assessed and contribute to a student's performance in each course.

Nonetheless, two salient characteristics accompany this instruction. First, although all four teachers are effective and experienced in teaching critical thinking, none of their classrooms operate in a quiet, efficient, highly organized manner. Instead, the road to completed tasks—particularly those requiring the construction rather than the reproduction of an answer—is often bumpy, circuitous, and unpredictable; it requires frequent midcourse correction. Managing the social conditions and cognitive demands of these critical thinking tasks is hard work, even for able teachers.

A second salient feature characterizes the work of the four teachers in this study: There are interactions in the classrooms of these four teachers that do not fit neatly into instructional categories; these are activities that neither directly explain a teacher's understanding of subject matter nor directly influence a student's performance assessment. Instead, these activities assist students in organizing thought. Most frequently, through discussion or demonstration, these activities provide reinforcement or elaboration of explanations introduced through other means. Some of these interactions are exercises that practice academic tasks, such as solving word problems similar to those found on exams. Others consist largely of discussion and listening activities; teachers intend these activities to build reasoning skills and to develop student ideas, which will later be used in a reasoning task. However, because these activities offer limited participation and lack the direct accountability associated with critical thinking tasks, few students draw upon reasoning skills while participating in them. Occasionally, a teacher inadvertently provides the procedures or formulas for response rather than coaching students as they reason their own response. These activities, in short, are not directly controlled by teachers and do not directly benefit student learning. Instead, these activities serve another purpose, to support and sustain participation in academic tasks.

For Bob, Langdon, Linda, and Conrad, designing academic tasks and presenting content is not enough to assure learning. These planning and narrative processes are only part of a teacher's responsibilities. While planning and narration do translate pedagogical content knowledge into academic tasks for students—they transpose subject matter understanding into the curriculum in place—this translation is not, in itself, sufficient; for meaningful learning to occur, teachers must also create environments in which students are willing to work.

All four teachers view managing critical thinking as integral and significant to their work, a skill that makes possible their work as subject matter specialists and curriculum designers. It is both a source of pride and frustration. In their interviews Bob, Langdon, Linda, and Conrad speak of students who are able to accomplish previously unsuccessful tasks and of the difficulty in motivating student interest in their courses, particularly in focusing the work of seniors at the end of the school year. They describe their teaching as subject matter understanding contained within well-managed academic tasks. They also speak of difficulties in their daily supervision of tasks and activities. Concepts need reteaching, important procedures need review, expectations need clarification, and time needs adjustment. In their classroom performance, Bob, Langdon, Linda, and Conrad use their pedagogical content knowledge to direct the conduct of these management tasks; images of games, battles, journeys, and magic also shape their understanding of this role.

MANAGING "THE GAME"

To generate ideas that contrast historical groups, Bob is playful in large and small group discussions. For example, in reviewing the political spectrum, he announces, "There are three ways in which the radical and reactionary perspectives are similar. Take three minutes to talk about one of these ideas with your partner." Later in the hour, he again uses paired discussion to develop an analogy between an automobile and the political spectrum. His instructions to students are these: "Some have said that the political spectrum is like a car. Take three and a half minutes and name the part of an automobile where you would locate the essence of liberalism, moderation, and conservatism." Both paired discussions on the political spectrum are designed to provide students with resource ideas to use in developing their major essay assignment, the letter comparing Adams and Wynkoop.

He inserts humorous asides into major discussion tasks to sustain student interest; the sources of this humor are shaped by his organizing imagery for teaching, the game. These light episodes establish the opposition necessary to teamwork. The majority of these comments are directed at himself, especially from his role as Mr. Jellyblob, but he also teases individuals and the group as a whole. Teachers, Mr. Jellyblob notes, are idiosyncratic and "always give substitutes bum instructions." Upon noticing Veronica gazing out the window, he asks, "Does Mr. Post let you look out the window like that? He must be really an easy fellow!" After Joseph added an important point to the discussion, Mr. Jellyblob observes, "Joseph, is it? Mr. Post didn't say you make helpful comments. He doesn't understand you." Since Bob's chalkboard handwriting and artwork are the subject of much discussion, Mr. Jellyblob could comment upon its recent improved clarity: "I imagine that Mr. Post doesn't print as well as that, does he?" Moreover, teachers also have humane strengths; they have memories and know their students well. "But you know something else I remember. I think I remember, back in the third grade, a slogan called 'No taxation without_____.' " Later, when commenting about Carin's consistent talking, Mr. Jellyblob compliments Bob: "Mr. Post was right on when he said that she's a talker."

Humor directed at individual students and the group also sustains student interest and brings attention back to the discussion. It is a reminder of the rules and regulations and the importance of playing well. Bob begins, as Mr. Jellyblob, by reviewing the substitute instructions: "They said when I come to class, watch out for certain students who tend to talk a lot. Like Carin Rader." Later, he stops Kerry's contribution: "I couldn't quite hear you because that girl in the back was talking." In reminding students of their freshman study of Marxist principles, he teases them about their advancing maturity: "And it's not exactly the kind of thing that young people ought to be learning, certainly as freshmen. Now I understand that you people are sophomores and you can look at dangerous ideas now." Having assigned the girls to discuss the first essay question and the boys to discuss the second, he teasingly challenges the boys to do well: "Mr. Post said that probably the girls will do a lot better job than the boys at explaining their essay questions." While reviewing the Stamp Act, he notes, "Now help the boys, because I'm sure they haven't thought about this yet." At the end of the discussion, he summarizes the work of the two groups; "Mr. Post was right. The boys must have slept last night." Humor establishes the game imagery and sustains discussion.

Bob's response to student comments in discussion takes the form of questioning for clarification or coaching through elaboration. In his role as Mr. Jellyblob, Bob accepts Joseph's dispute of the prediction that girls will perform more successfully in discussion. "I don't know. Mr. Post may have been wrong. But the question is—let's focus on that, please—'man is basically motivated by his economic self-interest.'" He frequently restates a student answer and asks for further explication, sometimes directed to the same student and sometimes directed to another. In the discussion about economic motivations for political actions, he uses this strategy frequently.

"Ok, but I'm still confused," Mr. Post continued. "Because it seems to me that what you're talking about, Veronica, is kind of like what Vicki was talking about earlier. But I'm still confused as to what we mean by 'economic self-interest.' Kerry do you have an answer to that?"

"Well, people are . . . people are concerned that their money, . . . I mean, that their profits or how they are going to be paying for it."

"Is this simply saying that people, that all of us—you and me and everyone else— is basically after the big bucks? Or the little bucks? Elizabeth?" Mr. Post questioned.

"Yes, I think that when it comes down to people doing anything it is because they're angry because they're losing money or because they're being stopped from making more money."

Through interchanges like this one, Bob is able to give students additional time for thinking about their responses and for explaining them more consistently and accurately. At the beginning of this discussion, student responses are relatively brief. Toward the end of the discussion, however, they are much more fully explained.

"Greg would say," Mr. Post started in again, "that since the Stamp Act was used by people without a major stake in society to increase their position, one could argue that it wasn't strictly economic. It involved something else. Susan?"

"Well, I agree with Greg—because they were using the fact that they were being taxed without representation as the . . . the principle was wrong and so they were using it as a basis to rebel. I mean, it wasn't really economic, but it was more the principle of the matter that they were being taxed without representation. And it meant that they were trying to gain more than lower taxes—it was their means of rebellion because they could gain more advantage and political power."

Through restatement, Bob encourages greater development of ideas in discussion.

Finally, to sustain student participation in discussion tasks, like a good coach, Bob must occasionally ignore irrelevant comments or correct inappropriate student behavior. It is Joseph's impertinence that is most often ignored. Joseph completes the greeting that Bob spoke into the intercom, comments that Lauren was "in trouble," suggests that the reading by Jensen was "about election bosses," and notes that Mr. Jellyblob's third grade education "sure was a long time ago." Each of these, while irrelevant to the topic, does show Joseph's attention to the discussion.

But not all interactions are playful. Bob also has to refocus attention of students who are not listening to the discussion. His is a particularly conversational group and he continually works to maintain their focus on history. As he explains his substitute role, Bob draws Christopher and Joseph back from reading *As You Like It* for their English class.

"Today, I want you to forget about me as teacher for a minute, although I will retain certain things. Like I'll look at somebody that's working on something else, Christopher. Today, I'm going to play the role of a substitute teacher. But I still retain my perogatives. So that if I see Joseph more interested in his Shakespeare, pray tell, than in our discussion today, I'll notice that."

And again, as he reads the essay question to be discussed, Bob brings Carin in: "That chatty one in the back—what did Mr. Post say? Carin?" He orders Joseph's consistent efforts to redirect the discussion and to negotiate an easier task for the day.

"All right, I hear tell that Mr. Post has given the wrong instructions here. It's the girls that are supposed to be able to explain Question A, is that correct?"

"Those are the wrong instructions. We're supposed to have a free period today." [Phil could play a role in this simulation.]

"Yes, you said teachers were always leaving wrong instructions." Joseph spoke up from the back of the room.

[Mr. Post-Jellyblob searched through his page of instructions.] " 'Watch out for the third row, fifth seat.' Oh, you're the one. I'm supposed to keep an eye on you, Joseph."

Managing this discussion is hard work for Bob; despite his years of experience, the social opportunities for peer attention and anxiety over expected intellectual risks require its continual monitoring and adjustment.

Bob uses a variety of strategies to provide students with confidence in accomplishing the two major written tasks in his curriculum: the essay exam and the letter writing assignment. Compared to interactions in discussion, these strategies are more specific routines, designed to give practice. His primary strategy is to use writing to generate ideas. To provide students with information, he expects notetaking during discussion. To open the class session on the day following the distribution of the Sam Adams letter assignment, Bob asks his students to summarize their task in this assignment in writing and to note the procedures they plan to follow. He also requires students to complete a written review assignment for each text chapter. In a journal of ideas about history, students try out ideas, state opinions, and explore relationships among ideas and events in a nonevaluative setting. Frequently these explorations are designed to be incorporated into the major writings. Journal Entry #16, for example, asks students to create a metaphor for the American Revolutionary Army that is better than the one presented in class discussion. The army could then become one possible illustrative event in the essay question.

A second strategy assists students in organizing their ideas. Bob sets aside class time for writing the introductory paragraph of this letter. During that ten minutes, he looks quickly over each writer's shoulder, then reminds students that, as Sam Adams, they are writing to a friend and must introduce Jeremiah Wynkoop at the beginning. After asking students to write the introduction to their letter, he reads an introductory paragraph he wrote. To assist students in developing their ideas, he outlines one possible organizing plan for comparing Adams and Wynkoop.

    I. Introduction
   II. Comparison Accenting Similarities
      A. Background
      B. Common Attitudes (colonial rights)
      C. Common Personal Attitudes (respect)
  III. Comparison Accenting Differences
      A. Business Experience and Background
      B. Attitudes Toward Colonial Actions (emphasis radical vs. moderate)
  IV. Reaffirm Sam Adams's Views

Finally, because of their diligence and difficulties with the assignment, Bob compromises on time: He postpones the Friday deadline until the following Monday.

In presenting this organizational model, Bob's intention is to stimulate the further development of ideas. But some of his students accept the plan as their routine; it is an algorithm to follow. A section of Keith's paper is an example:

As you've already known, I was born and raised in a poor family and even until today I was still poor. But, unlike me, J. Wynkoop was born of rich, middle-class parents, and before he became an adult, he had already inherited a profitable business upon the sudden death of his father. With such a head start in society, he rapidly achieved a notable success in commerce. Before I continue, my friend, I would like you to know that I felt no envy toward Mr. Wynkoop's wealth, because I feel a politician should represent his people and work for his people, and one's own wealth should be the last thing to come to a politician's mind. So I hope you can understand that I haven't really failed financially because I've never taken money seriously.

To continue, remember in the previous paragraph I stated that both Mr. Wynkoop's and my attitude toward colonial rights were very much similar? Well, they are and still I expect that the action that we plan to take here is almost opposite. For example, Mr. Wynkoop believed that an American should possess all the rights of an Englishman, but when these rights are unduly provoked by the Stamp Act, he simply suggested that we make peaceful appeals to Britain and let Britain repeal the Stamp Act. However, I believe it was Mr. Wynkoop's luck that the British Parliament finally repealed the hateful measure. But what caught me most by surprise was his reaction toward the Declaratory Act. He said, and I quote, "It was not more than a bravely flying banner designed to cover a dignified retreat from an untenable position." Now can you believe that? . . .

Keith follows the outline given by discussing similar backgrounds and common attitudes, then by comparing differences in business experience, background, and attitudes. As a result, the model writing made this task predictable rather than challenging. It organizes his thinking rather than challenging it.

Coach Bob manages the tension between instructional and organizational concerns through humor, correction, and practice. He teases students and pokes fun at himself in order to keep student attention on critical thinking tasks. Balancing this lighthearted atmosphere, he also provides progressively difficult practice and continued elaboration of ideas. His organizing image provides a useful metaphor for these negotiations.

MANAGING "THE BATTLE"

In Langdon's classroom, the battle appears in discussion activities that, like academic tasks, challenge assumptions about democratic and authoritarian forms of government and that require an understanding of opposing political views. Here, he uses four strategies to sustain student interest: repetition and clarification, student questioning, humor, and correction. Langdon's most common strategy in sustaining discussion is to repeat a student answer before developing ideas further. This repetition serves both to keep students involved in the discussion and to provide rest before the next day. The recitation sometimes becomes an echoing chorus, with group rather than individual response. This is the case when discussing the composition of the Electoral College.

"The State Republican Committee," Mr. Selhorst began again, "in a process completely separate from the delegate process, picks the electors. And how many electors does each state get?"

David continued. "As many as Congressmen and Senators they have."

"That's right. As many members of the House of Representatives and Senate they have. So therefore, California gets how many?"

"Forty-seven," came back the chorus.

"Forty-seven. And Nevada gets . . . "

"Three," responded the chorus.

"Three. Why does Nevada get one Congressman?"

"Because of the population."

This time the chorus is not quite accurate and Langdon corrects the response in his repetition. "Because the Constitution requires that every state get one Congressman regardless of population." This pattern becomes Langdon's form of feedback to students and occurs more than twenty times in one hour-long discussion.

Langdon also solicits student-generated questions to maintain involvement, his second strategy. The questions produced during discussion are largely about content that is not yet clearly understood. Langdon promotes this inquiry explicitly and directly. He regularly stops between sections of a presentation to allow time for questions and their responses before continuing. This builds courage for the battle. Ted, for example, is held more accountable for the statement of his question about the nominating process than for its particular content. "How they . . . when they have the convention and they are putting together their candidate, I didn't understand . . . exactly how they can upset all the delegates and have an open convention." Once the question is worded accurately—"Are you talking about the Carter-Kennedy dispute?"—the response and review was opened to all students. In the course of one review session, questioning of this nature occurs thirteen times.

Langdon's use of humor is more impersonal than that of the other three teachers; it is directed entirely outward and does not include himself. It is also more biting, designed to instill order and discipline in his classroom. He asks for "a victim-volunteer" to give quick reviews and calls on students as volunteers: "How kind of you, Miss Baird, to volunteer." He teases the girls by pointing out that Jefferson's criteria for enfranchisement did not include women. With the lowered voting age, Langdon notes that "we now allow children to vote in this country." And he finds that "it just doesn't pay to give seniors a break." His long dissertation on David's performance and Sergio's cap is designed to bring David and Sergio back into the discussion and to focus these seniors' attention on the importance of working consistently until the end of the semester. To keep student attention, Langdon regularly includes these humorous asides and supports student-generated humor that is pertinent.

Like humor, correcting inappropriate behavior and responses also promotes the order and discipline needed in battle. At the beginning of each class hour, Langdon checks the accuracy of his attendance records. Because students have three days to clear an absence, he frequently reviews his records for the past week as well as for the day before. Students with unexcused absences are informed about the effect of the attendance upon performance.

"Miss Koeninger, step up here to the podium, please. . . . Tiny, what about last Monday? . . . Mark, you'll have to get a duplicate for me. . . . Emily? Please bring it tomorrow. . . . Hanneman? That's a cut." [He also chides boys who wear sunglasses until they are stowed out of sight.]

Langdon's corrections, however, are not limited to inappropriate behavior. He also corrects inaccuracies in student thinking during discussion. When Tom guesses that one votes for delegates instead of presidential candidates on election day, he is corrected. "No, you're not pulling the handle for delegates. You're pulling the handle for—electors. Don't get the delegates, who are the people that go to the nominating convention, confused with the electors, who vote for president." When Greg hypothesizes that the rationale for a two-party system is to anticipate the faults in the major party, Langdon cautions him to listen carefully to the question. "You're not answering my question. You're anticipating the question." In developing one point about the fundamental difference between the Republican and Democratic parties, Langdon repeats his question three times.

"*Question*: What is the difference between the Republicans and the Democrats . . . the *basic* difference?"

David was back. "They're conservative."

"That's not the most fundamental difference," Mr. Selhorst retorted. "Their platforms do tend to be different, but they tend to be different because of a more fundamental cause."

"One is more conservative and one more liberal?" Ted spoke up.

"Ba-loney!"

"Well, that's what they say."

"I know that. It's not that it's untrue; it's just that that's the effect, not the cause. You are looking at superficial things. I want to know what the basic difference is between the Republicans and the Democrats that is not subject to inflamatory terms, like 'liberals' and 'conservatives.' "

"Isn't it just that each takes a different position on issues?"

"Look at it. Right there before your eyes," [Mr. Selhorst pointed to his diagram on the board.] "What difference do the factions make that make up the Democratic Party?"

But not all of Langdon's strategies place students on the offensive. His primary strategy during written tasks is to provision students with information and assistance. Like Bob, Langdon supports student achievement through providing all major questions at the beginning of the unit. In addition, for each unit, he supplies students with four to eight pages of supporting explanation. These materials illustrate major principles or concepts or supply background information for discussion of those concepts. For example, materials for the unit, "The Political Spectrum in Theory and Practice," include a statement of underlying assumptions, a comparison of democratic and authoritarian positions in theory and in practice, a "ship of state" analogy, an illustration of dialectic progession in history, and a chronology of American political parties. Langdon also arranges conference times; during these Thursday help sessions at lunch, during sixth period, or after school, students can raise questions about the written task or clarify the relations of ideas. Langdon sees an average of twelve students a week in these conferences.

On occasion, however, when furnishing this information Langdon transposes an academic task into a routine. Although the unit exam question appears to be one requiring the assembly of several complex ideas into a unified whole, Langdon, in fact, provides the essay organization and illustrative example.

"I'm specifically asking you in that five points to explain the political spectrum and to define the terms so that you can then move to a ten-point discussion of the Grand Inquisitor as a case study of the values of the far right. And as you move through these, if you find a value that cannot be illustrated by the example of the Grand Inquisitor, you may use Hitler or Mussolini or the Ku Klux Klan or any other right-wing example. I just want to make sure that you know what the core values of the right are. And I want you to use specific illustrations.

"There is a fifteen-point discussion of the values of the left in theory, which is Marxism. And the reason for that is that I think you will discover that Marxism is inherently more complex and will take more time, and that's why the allocation of points. Then there is a five-point discussion on the discrepancy between the democratic values and authoritarian values. That I leave to your own study. And then there is a fifteen-point discussion on the two-party system in the United States."

In addition to prescribing the organization by supplying the point values, Langdon suggests through his evaluation system that the essay assignment is, instead, a series of short paragraphs. Each section becomes a separate problem requiring the reproduction of known information.

Langdon reduces the risk of failure by supplying students with a wide variety of information and time for discussing it. To generate ideas for the great debate, students take notes during discussion. They listen to Langdon's presentations during a unit and copy his notes from the board verbatim. Because each of the weekly written assignments is directly related to a section of the exam question, those written assignments become another source of ideas and organization for the exam. Langdon discusses all weekly assignments and all major topics of the essay question prior to testing. He also monitors time carefully. Because of his absence, he postpones the Friday exam until Monday in order to complete the discussion.

Like the others, Langdon's strategies to maintain critical thinking tasks are colored by his organizing imagery: He interjects into the debate humor directed at individuals and groups; his response to student participation, at times by answering questions and at times by repeating student comments, instills the discipline needed for battle; he solicits student involvement through regular opportunities for questions; he corrects inappropriate behavior and imprecise thinking; and he provides necessary information and training. Like the others, he finds that monitoring student cooperation and encouraging participation in these tasks require his constant attention. Of the four, Langdon's battle image places the most stress on the oppositional purposes of teachers and students. Those students who enter classroom negotiations must be prepared for the debate.

MANAGING "THE JOURNEY"

Journeys require intermittent rest periods to restore energy or gather meaning before traveling on. Therefore, Linda makes extensive use of discussion and demonstrations in her classroom to provide this reflection. Sometimes these discussions attend to careful reading and interpretation of line. After reading *King Lear*, for example, Linda asked students to interpret the cause of Lear's death and the meaning of the final events. She focused first on a speech by Edgar about Kent by reading aloud the passage:

Whilst I was big in clamour, came there a man,
Who, having seen me in my worst estate,
Shunn'd my abhorr'd society; but then, finding
Who"twas that so endur'd, with his strong arms
He fastened on my neck, and bellowed out
As he'd burst heaven; threw him on my father;
Told the most piteous tale of Lear and him
That ever ear receiv'd; which in recounting
His grief grew puissant, and the strings of life
Began to crack (V, iii, 208–217).

She paused, then continued the questioning: "Who is this man? And why is Edgar moved by his tale?"

A second passage identifies the Duke of Albany's final act. Again, Linda picked up her book and read:

> Our present business
> Is general woe. . . . Friends of my soul, you twain
> Rule in this realm, and the gor'd state sustain (V, iii, 318–320).

Linda took off her glasses, looked over her students, and commented, "At the end, Albany gives his kingdom to Kent and Edgar. Why Adrienne?"

On occasion, discussion demands a wider range of interpretation. Following a discussion of the the final act, Linda asks: "What do the characters in this play represent? Let's start with the two most tragic characters, Lear and Gloucester. What do they represent?"

Small group discussions also generate ideas for the journey. One morning Linda divides her students into groups of four; each group has a different general question and ten minutes to develop an oral response, applying it to Lear. Group I discusses this question: "From a novel or play of literary merit, select an important character who is a villain. Then, in a well-organized essay, analyze the nature of the character's villainy and show how it enhances meaning in the work."

Similarly, students are accountable both for listening actively and for recording ideas from discussion. On two occasions Linda asks students to review a previous discussion by reporting from their notes: One Thursday, they recalled the qualities represented by characters from Lear, which were noted in Wednesday's discussion, before concluding the final discussion of the play; as an introduction to *The Bear*, they reread biblical allusions presented as background for first semester readings. Her directions are these: "What I would like for you to do is to check back in your notes to see if you can find some of these characters—Isaac, Jacob and Esau, and Moses—that we've already talked about."

Three primary strategies sustain discourse on Linda's journey. Like Bob and Langdon, Linda uses humor to maintain student interest in the assigned task. Like Bob, her humor is directed toward self, the group and individuals, and occasionally toward the subject; she also supports student-generated humor, which maintains interest. Just as humor is less a part of a difficult but rewarding journey, Linda's humor is more subtle and less pervasive than in the other two classrooms; humor is less a part of a difficult but rewarding journey. She jokes about her position as an underpaid, older teacher: "I don't get paid much, but I do get paid"; and "it will probably help me if I put my new glasses on, since the print is so small." She settles students at the beginning of their practice AP exam by agreeing that "it is a silly thing to do on a Tuesday morning" and encourages them to take a little extra time so the campus will not be flooded with "screaming seniors" before the lunch hour. Her students receive a bonus on their essays for "being diligent and for having tired-looking eyes." She teases Gordon for wearing a wool sweater in 90 degree weather; Paul is already "out of the school-groove and no longer used to doing homework every night"; Nathan, who labeled absent students as "skippers," is cruel, with "a streak I hadn't seen before"; and "poor Paul is sitting over there groaning and moaning about having an assignment" during spring vacation. Literature is also the target of her gentle humor. *The Bear* is "one of those strange books" that cannot be read episodically: "You can't put it down and then immediately pick back up and start right where you left off. You almost always have to go back a page, two pages, sometimes three pages."

Student-generated humor in Linda's classroom is equally gentle and supportive. It is usually designed to release tensions generated during the performance of complex tasks. Student comments about the anticipated difficulty in reading *The Bear* are typical. Heather is going through "paper withdrawal" and is having difficulty thinking about the next assignment; Paul is grateful that the reading is "a short one"; Gordon turns back two or three pages "to where the sentence starts"; and Heather hopes to escape helping at home with "Wait, Mom, let me just finish this sentence." Patti expresses frustration with Faulkner's style: "It does make you wonder about a teacher's thoughts in assigning this!" Heather teases Nathan for changing his mind about the difficulty of the reading; but Nathan rolls his eyes at the thought of becoming a Faulkner addict. Each of these humorous asides serves to relieve tension and sustain interest.

As a second strategy for sustaining discussion, Linda makes it a point to respond initially to all student inquiries, even when the question is non-germane, in order to prevent discouragement. During the proofreading session for their Lear papers and an introductory presentation on *The Bear*, this is particularly true. When Rob asks if his absent classmates had additional time for writing, she begins a review of her grading policy. When Claire approaches with one more question about semicolons, even though Linda is introducing *The Bear*, she stops to look at the sentence and notes that the semicolon corrected the comma splice. When Trish, who was still filling out a book card, breaks in to ask the author of the text, Linda answers. When she is establishing the chronological relationship between reading assignments, Gordon interrupts to inquire when *King Lear* was written. Heather asks whether it was vocabulary that made reading Faulkner difficult. When Linda is identifying a two-page long sentence, Janis interposes to identify its end. When Nathan reviews briefly the biblical story of Abraham and Isaac, Paul asks who Benjamin was. Paul clarifies the necessity of distinguishing between *The Bear* and *Go Down, Moses* on the AP exam. Linda replies to each of these questions before returning to her presentation and this respectful response is the most salient of her strategies for maintaining student interest.

As a third strategy in discussion, she ignores or corrects occasional digressions. Those questions to which she responds, although frequently peripherial to the discussion, are nonetheless related to the task. Those she ignores or corrects are unrelated or erroneous. When Rob interrupts to ask when the *King Lear* books were to be collected, his question is ignored. When Paul asks the advantage of Faulkner's long sentence structure, his question is ignored. Heather's moaning at being responsible for biblical allusions is ignored. When Janis asks how long it took Faulkner to write a two-page sentence, her question is ignored. When Heather teases Nathan for conceding that Faulkner was no more difficult than Joyce, her comments are ignored. During the brief review of biblical allusions, Heather asks, "Who was Rachel?" Although Linda answered briefly, she adds that Rachel was irrelevant to this novel, and "Let's not digress here." Nathan suggests that "Ike" was short for "Ichabod." Although his classmates found Nathan's comment humorous, Linda continues the discussion, correcting first Nathan and later Paul.

"Isaac. Not Ichabod. Isaac. Now, Paul, who was Isaac?"

"He was the son of Abraham who was the sacrifice . . . the kid who was sacrificed, basically." [Paul began the review of material from last semester.]

"He was not . . . "

"Almost sacrificed." [Paul understood the correction.] "Abraham took him up to the mountain by God's order, and it was God's test of Abraham. Whether he would do it or not."

Linda's discussion strategies coach her students to continue the long, difficult journey. They help students to understand the path to successful literary analysis.

Where discussion activities can restore energy and provide reflection, reading assignments develop the understanding necessary for literary journeys. Although each of the four teachers assigned reading tasks, only Linda provides a strategy to sustain student efforts in challenging reading. When introducing Faulkner's *The Bear*, she is careful to bridge the gap between the familiar and the novel and is honest about the difficulty in approaching Faulkner's style. She notes, first of all, the change in historical period: "I'm asking you to make a giant shift from the beginning of the seventeenth century to the middle of the twentieth." She also notes that Faulkner's style is similar to another more familiar, twentieth century author. "If I can draw a parallel to something you've read before, he's closer probably to Conrad in *The Heart of Darkness* than to anything you have read up to this point."

To explain the relationships between sound and meaning on these journeys, Linda provides a variety of auditory and visual experiences. She reads Shakespeare's blank verses, both in discussing *King Lear* and in reviewing identification quizzes. She reads poetry selections with rhythm and meaning. And, as she introduces students to Faulkner, she reads pages of *The Bear* so they can hear the cadence of prepositional phrases and participles: "You have to read it with your ear," she warns. Sometimes these readings are combined with visual forms, as in a filmed performance of Lear. There, the sounds of Shakespearean language, the weathering of elements, the power of the storm, the use of light and shadow, and musical background convey the underlying emotions of sibling rivalry and intergenerational conflict.

In addition to connecting this new work with a familiar one, Linda is honest about the difficulty in reading Faulkner and provides specific suggestions designed to sustain students' efforts in this difficult task.

"*This* is going to be the most difficult reading assignment you've done since you've been in high school. But what I'm going to do today is get you started with *The Bear*. I'm going to give you some help.... I'm going to make a couple of suggestions about how to read Faulkner. And what will help you—since you have had no experience in reading Faulkner before—what will help you the most is if you will read the book, the entire *The Bear*, over the vacation. If you will read the whole thing once—read it straight through in one sitting—that's the easiest way to read Faulkner. And you'll see why when I read a little bit with you today. His style is both marvelous and incredibly difficult. It requires, at the least, a tremendous *reading* ability."

She alerts students to the lengthy sentence structure by pointing out a two-page sentence. She points out that this novella was originally published as one of three books in *Go Down, Moses*. She provides study questions to guide reading and points out important sections in each section of the novella. Because this is "one of those strange books" with a complex literary style, she suggests reading aloud to someone. In the end, she suggests that although the first reading assignment will not be made until after vacation, an initial reading during vacation will put students "a long way ahead." Through these specific suggestions, Linda anticipates the difficulty her students will have with this reading assignment and provides an entry into the task that will make the strange familiar and reduce the intellectual risk in the actual assignment.

Linda, who relies most heavily on written tasks to develop understanding, regularly provides three kinds of strategies in managing these student activities. In developing the essay on *King Lear*, students check their progress with her several times before proceeding. Their journeys are divided into well-defined segments. Some of these conferences are held during class time; most, however, occur outside of class hours. Linda alerts students to this assistance in her course prospectus: "Your instructor is very anxious to make this a challenging and helpful course. If students do not understand an assignment and need extra help, they may come in before school, at lunch, or after school for assistance." Linda also provides a written reminder of students' accountability for the essay. Journeys contain certain hazards that warrant attention. This sheet outlines the importance of the thesis, mechanical considerations students should keep in mind, specific information about format for quotations used in the essay, and reminders about the paper format and value.

A second strategy, the most time-consuming in terms of class time, is peer editing. Just prior to submitting the Lear paper, Linda paired her students for proofreading. Their purpose is to discover careless mistakes in punctuation, commas, and sentence structure. The peer editor's task is to note the errors and to suggest corrections to the author. The author's task is to correct the identified errors before submitting the paper. Linda assists in this logical analysis. When Patti questions her about one comma, she responds, "Yes, that's ok because it's a long, introductory participial phrase. It isn't absolutely required, but when you've got a very long participial phrase, it helps to make things clear." To Nathan she replies, "I don't think 'purgation' is the word you mean there. I think what you meant is 'ex-purgate.' " To Gordon she adds, "No, it's a semicolon there, not a colon. That's a good sentence, but it might be better with a semicolon—because that's an independent clause." A few students, like Andrea, question the judgments of their editors and seek arbitration from Linda. Linda teases these students.

> [She studied the sentence Andrea questioned.] "This sentence. We've got to figure out . . . yes, she's setting off an appositive, 'Gloucester.' It's an interrupting element there. But why am I telling you?"
>
> "This is my paper," Andrea confessed.
>
> "Oh, cheat-cheat-cheat!" Ms. Reed teased her for having taken her own paper back.
>
> "That's what you get!" Trish bantered.

Although Linda announces a ten-minute limit for editing, she adjusts the time by the diligence of her students and by individual need. She does not, in fact, collect papers until twenty-five minutes have passed and permits Claire and Marc to continue reviewing their essays during the next activity.

Linda's strategies in managing the Advanced Placement writing tasks are more systematic and sequential. Here she provides a sequence of activities that are increasingly closer approximations of the examination. At the beginning of the year, these rapid literary analysis tasks represent a novel kind of writing to her students; none of their previous literature classes had required them. To help students prepare for these assignments, Linda stresses discussion, close textual analysis, vocabulary skills, and reading quizzes. To develop the actual skills of literary analysis, Linda first presents these tasks as a group assignment and discusses the procedure while writing their collective response on a projected transparency. The second assignment is completed in small groups, with each group producing a response. The third analysis is an out-of-class assignment, to be completed without time restrictions. By the fourth assignment, students are ready to respond to the question individually as an in-class assignment. The questions for these analyses are taken from previous years' AP tests. To prepare for the actual AP exam, students take a four-hour practice AP exam, based upon the previous year's questions. These assignments help students to bridge the gap between their prior experience and the expectations of the exam; each step in the progression requires greater cognitive independence from students. Their progression is sustained by the confidence developed in mastering past steps.

Linda's journey embraces both rigor and reflection. She manages critical thinking tasks with close reading, humor, correction, cooperation, and carefully designed sequences.

MANAGING "THE MAGIC"

To encourage hypothesis generation, confirmation, and clarification in discussion and problem sets, Conrad expresses puzzlement at mysterious principles and stresses the skillful manipulation of a wide variety of information. Five strategies characterize Conrad's management of discussion tasks. First, Conrad uses humor, a part of his magical Physics-land image, to interject variety into discussions. His most frequent humorous topics were the subject of physics and himself. The optical spectrum is a "little pimply part of the entire electromagnetic spectrum." In color vision theory, black, which "tickles none of the cones on your retina," is "the essence of the Happy Donut." When overhead lights are out during the lightbox demonstration, he has difficulty seeing the filters in the dark "which I guess is another physics principle." He jumps at the heat generated by the working lightbox. An alternate physics book is old, "I mean *old.* . . . Nineteen-fifty-nine old." He satirizes his own clumsiness in demonstrations: "this doesn't happen on TV" comments on how the lightbox is not quite ready for the demonstration; looking for filters in the dark may cost "all my color vision"; moving rapidly from the lightbox to the chalkboard and back provides "my exercise today and [I] may not need those sit-ups." Conrad kids the group about its expertise in color mixing.

"You see those poor artists. We're going to get some basics about light in our heads, in an hour, and will be able to walk over there and tell any of those people who have been there four years why mixing this and this becomes that. Are we a trip?"

He ties a gentle teasing of individual students to the concept under discussion. He plays with Charlie Long's last name in describing the wavelength of red light; with Laura Black's last name, which represents a color that does not "tickle" retinal cones; with "boring" students, like Susan, who confer about computations before school; and with Daniel, who thinks color adjustments in a television are "cool, closer to fantasies of L.A."

Conrad supports student-generated humor that contributes to his Physics-land imagery or sustains student interest. He transforms his praise of Randy's scholarship into an Oscar ceremony by asking, "And who would you like to thank?" Laura hisses at the play on her last name and the nothingness of black light. When her classmates giggle at the pun, Conrad compares the joke to "the essence of the Happy Donut." Randy adds a counterpoint to a short hummed tune inserted into the color mixing demonstration. Each of these humorous asides contributes to one of Conrad's goals for students and sustains student attention on important physical concepts.

Second, he responds to student comments by using those ideas, by asking for clarification, or by suggesting clearer reasoning. "Yes," he notes in response to Bill's statement about green light. "It's green light mixed with red light that makes yellow light." Randy remembers that the three primary colors are symbolized in the logo of a Sony television: "You're right. I hadn't thought of that, but you do make your color adjustments with these three lights." When Lee explains that subtracting red light from blue light results in black light: "Ah, see that—you guys figured all this stuff out before I could tell you about it. You're really disappointing me!" He asks Russell to explain why adding blue to yellow will produce white light. When John guesses rather than hypothesizing, Conrad suggests that "what we might all want to do before answering is to think." But when John explains the existence of blue and yellow shadows in the lightbox, Conrad adds to his explanation. "You see . . . one stick, but the lights back there are in different locations. So when the stick blocks out the blue, it isn't combining the blue with the yellow." Nonetheless, despite his goal of asking students for clarification of their thinking, Conrad's more typical response is to repeat and elaborate upon a student response.

Third, Conrad encourages students to interject questions and comments into his presentations and demonstrations, and he stops to respond to these before proceeding, even when the question is related to an aside. One Friday, he digresses from a review of angstrom units in the optical spectrum to speculate on the prehistorical development of technology.

"People didn't have words—well, I guess they had words before they had letters. They couldn't write letters before they had numbers. And they didn't have much in numbers until they invented what? The *zero*. Oh, moving right long, I'm off on my rocker again."

Laura spoke up quickly. "Where did fire come into that?"

"And we have 4,000 angstrom units. . . . "

"Where do fire and the wheel come into that?" Laura insisted.

"I don't know. I don't think we invented fire. I think we just picked it up on a stick. You know, seriously, you don't think cave men understood fire?!"

The mention of the history of technology is an aside with magical properties, designed to hold attention rather than to develop further the concept of angstrom units. After a demonstration of color subtraction, John admits, "I don't understand. How does black come in?" Conrad responds to this inquiry by reteaching the principle of filtering and the properties of the cyan, magenta, and yellow filters.

A fourth strategy Conrad uses to sustain student interest in discussion is ignoring or correction. Some of the ignored comments are irrelevant asides. He ignores Russell's question about the mixing of colors in a filter, John's observation that the yellow light looks like malaria, Susan's comment that a hot lightbox smells like cow's milk, and Russell's prediction that the stick would be used in the next demonstration. Other disregarded comments are answers to his questions that contain faulty thinking. After demonstrating the color mixing in cyan and yellow, Conrad asks:

> "Well, let's see, are there any other ways of taking three colors, two at a time?"
>
> "Well, yellow and . . . ," said Juli.
>
> "Red and . . . ," Melanie suggested.
>
> "White minus . . . ," Debbi offered.
>
> "Red and blue," Charlie concluded.
>
> "Red and blue looks like the only other combination that's possible that's here," Mr. Rizzo commented.

Conrad chooses not to correct Juli, Melanie, and Debbi for guessing rather than using reasoning; his silence does not embarrass them and sustains their efforts.

Finally, although Conrad is usually supportive and positive, even lenient, in relations with students, he can be quite sharp when students demonstrate immaturity. He corrects determined efforts to delay the discussion and inappropriate talking during demonstration. When Susan asked how pre-historic people discovered fire, Conrad's response is a sharp hyperbole: "When we get into anthropology during the middle of the summer, I recommend 'quest for fire'; I recommend 'biological time bomb'; there are several other topics I can recommend to you at a later time. OK? Moving right along." He then returns to a discussion of wavelength separation. As he summarized the principles of the lightbox demonstration, Conrad notices John talking to Chan. He stops mid-sentence, excuses himself while stepping to John's side, and speaks in a low, clear voice: "I'm going to punch you in the mouth." John stops talking immediately, and Conrad returns to the lightbox at the center of the room to continue his summarization. These corrections are far from prevalent in maintaining student order, but they are one of five strategies Conrad chooses to use in sustaining student attention in discussion tasks.

To acquire a base for magical speculations, Conrad asks students to observe, read, and listen. Reading activities prepare students for lab work. On the day prior to each lab, Conrad assigns a lab worksheet as text. Students are to read carefully and to identify the lab's purpose and procedures. He provides information for generating hypotheses through listening, observing, and notetaking skills. Demonstrations in Conrad's classroom allow students to pursue irresistible speculations. During a discussion of color mixing, he holds two filters up to the light, a red and a blue, and asks students to predict what color will result. After illustrating the difference between color addition and color subtraction, one student checks his understanding with another example:

"If you mix cyan and yellow together," Charlie asked, "would you get green?"

"You'd get who?" Mr. Rizzo responded.

"You'd get green."

"If you put cyan and yellow light together, would you get green?" Mr. Rizzo repeated.

"Because it's like each category on the list. Cyan takes away red and yellow takes away the blue, but you still have green left."

"What are you predicting, Charlie?"

"That we'd have green left."

"Charlie's predicting that we get a green. Let's do it on the board and see how it works. Charlie says if I have a cyan filter and I shine white light through it, I'm going to take away red. That's what the cyan filter is going to do. And the yellow filter that I use is going to take away blue. So what I should be left with from the white light is what? Green. This is Charlie's prediction."

By asking Charlie to explain how he arrived at this prediction, Conrad is able to determine the logic of Charlie's hypothesis and to support Charlie's confidence in his hypothesis. He also expects students to listen to his explanations and to take notes on key ideas.

Although Conrad's written tasks are the shortest of the four teachers, he uses equally varied strategies to maintain them. Here, he supports student learning on problem sets, tests, and lab reports. First, to build student confidence in problem solving skills, he provides students with clues and feedback as they work on word problems. As he assigns a set of problems from the text, he dictates the answers. Then, as students work independently on these sets, they compare their answers to those given and determine immediately the correctness of their formulas. This feedback also directs their participation during discussion of a problem set: Having identified areas of difficulty, students can attend to the discussion of some problems as confirmation of their understanding and to the discussion of others for clarification in reasoning.

Further, Conrad encourages students to develop scientific confidence through seeking assistance. He meets with students individually to discuss problems or grades. He announces these conferences in the course syllabus.

> In general I will be glad to meet with you whenever the need arises. . . . Since I cannot physically meet with each of you on the spur of the moment and discuss your grade at length, please see me before or after class, during the passing periods, before school (7:50 a.m.), or when I am not in a meeting, to schedule an appointment.

He also urges students to share information about problem solving among themselves. At the beginning of the year, only three students could help others with the problems when homework was reviewed in class; by May considerably more can supply explication. Because of the interconnectedness of problems on a physics test, during the exam Conrad will "sell" an answer to one question that has impact upon the solution to several others. He finds that this builds a student's confidence in completing the exam. At the first of the year, many students "bought" answers by paying with a lowered possible score; in May their confidence level has increased to the point that no students are interested in a purchase.

Finally, Conrad carefully phrases questions to clarify thinking and build confidence. During lab sessions, he helps students transform their observations and data into formulas to be solved. His queries—"What is the question?" "What do you need to know?" "How do you get that?" "How do you set up the equation?"—focus more on understanding the problem than on actual mathematical calculations. Because most real physics problems are stated as ill-structured situations that need solving rather than as formulas, Conrad assigns only word problems. For example:

> 14. The dimensions of the picture on a slide are 6.4 cm by 7.6 cm. This slide is to be projected to form an image 1.5 m by 1.8 m at a distance of 9.0 m from the objective lens of the projector. (a) What is the distance from the slide to the objective lens? (b) What focal length objective lens must be used? (Williams et al., 1972, p. 349).

To increase performance on unit tests, Conrad phrases questions in discussion and on the tests themselves so that the problems correspond to formulas emphasized in class.

Conrad uses magic as entertaining elaboration during discussion and demonstrations and to lighten students' anxiety about subject matter. Useful in sustaining interest, it appears especially as humorous asides during discussion and demonstration, and supports student speculation; it is less useful in correcting inappropriate behavior because it does not communicate the seriousness of Conrad's intent in those situations. His strategies for sustaining attention to written tasks—primarily providing answers to problem sets and "selling" exam questions—are equally imaginative but uncolored by the magical imagery.

CLASSROOM CULTURES

Creating classroom environments where learning can occur, monitoring and sustaining group activities, is thus central to the work of teachers. The relative difficulty in establishing classroom culture depends upon the social context of the tasks assigned to students, within which teachers and students interact. As teachers increase the cognitive challenge—that is, as the intellectual space between the known and novel aspects of a task widen—students accelerate demands for self-direction as they press for predictability and routine. Teachers, therefore, must not only provide explanation of content and design tasks for learning, but they must also manage student anxiety about failure and establish mores that promote participation but do not reduce cognitive goals. The teachers in this study together use varying combinations of eighteen strategies to sustain critical thinking tasks.

Despite individual pedagogical content knowledge and organizing imagery, all four teachers in this study employ six strategies that order these classroom tensions. These shared strategies are the conventions of classrooms. They appear to represent traditional patterns of teacher behavior in classrooms, regardless of teacher or discipline.

1. Using writing to learn
2. Discussing major topics thoroughly
3. Interjecting humor to lighten otherwise serious work
4. Responding supportively to student comments
5. Ignoring incongruous student responses
6. Correcting erroneous thinking

Although the implementation of these six conventions assumes an individual cast in each classroom, the four teachers use these behaviors to build a sense of community and fun. Bob and Langdon assign writing activities as a part of larger tasks. Bob requires a journal of ideas about history where students can explore concepts in a nonevaluative setting. These entries become sources of ideas for other written assignments or for discussion. He also assigns "brain fertilizers" to generate ideas. Linda's loosely structured essay assignment and Langdon's weekly written assignments serve this same purpose. All four teachers encourage notetaking during presentations, discussions, and demonstrations. All four also use discussion to clarify and supplement the text. Bob reviews topics for the exam questions. Langdon clarifies the distinction between the nomination and election processes. Conrad focuses upon physics topics explained inadequately in the text. And Linda discusses character, interpretation, and theme in *King Lear*. These teachers create fun through teasing students, individually and as a group, and capturing the humorous aspects of the content or assigned activities. In addition, all but Langdon poke fun at themselves. Conrad, Linda, and Bob use student ideas, ask for clarification, and suggest clearer reasoning. Langdon repeats, sometimes echoes, short student responses and questions to clarify thinking. All ignore irrelevant asides. Conrad disregards responses containing faulty thinking. Linda sometimes ignores extraneous comments. All are careful to provide corrective feedback in discussion. Linda corrects Paul's review of the story of Abraham. Langdon counters Tom's explanation of the election process and reminds Greg to listen carefully to the question before answering. Bob corrects Tony's misunderstanding of Rossiter's position on the Declaration of Independence. Conrad corrects Bill's confusion of light and pigment. These teachers understand that when students have difficulty and make mistakes, they do not stop learning but create their own, sometimes creative and sometimes false, solution strategies. This is why incorrect answers from students are not per se obstructions in the course of a lesson but constitute an essential object of their work.

Beyond these conventional behaviors, however, each teacher exhibits a different combination of strategies for organizing classroom events. At least in these four teachers, this configuration of classroom mores represents the fundamental moral views each teacher holds about teaching and learning. Each has selected five, six, or seven behaviors from this list of twelve:

1. Providing individual assistance for students
2. Using peer support
3. Soliciting student questions
4. Correcting inappropriate behavior
5. Distributing essay questions prior to testing
6. Altering deadlines to allow adequate preparation
7. Providing immediate feedback
8. Clarifying expectations for final products
9. Using progress checks at key intervals in a major task
10. Sequencing a series of activities to move from the known to the novel
11. Modeling effective performance
12. Phrasing questions to clarify thinking and build confidence

The organizing imagery drawn from their understanding of content and pedagogy influences, to varying degrees, each teacher's understanding of this configuration.

Bob uses five of these strategies in coaching the game of history. (a) He models good writing through presenting one possible organizing plan for a letter-essay and reading his imaginative introduction to the letter. (b) He uses the teamwork of paired discussions to generate ideas about historical principles. (c) He presents a game plan, the essay exam questions, at the beginning of a unit so students can focus their study. (d) Pressed by the mutability of the schedule during competency testing, he delays the completion of the letter writing asignment to permit thorough discussion. (e) Finally, he regularly corrects inappropriate behavior through inserting names of inattentive or misbehaving students into his explanations. Like an organized coach, Bob builds community values of teamwork, hard work, precise training, and time; motivated by these values, his students participate in daily workouts.

In managing the battle of politics and government, Langdon uses seven strategies. (a) He provides immediate feedback by discussing the weekly written assignment directly upon its completion. (b) He reminds students of the criteria for evaluating major tasks by providing the point value of each section of the unit essay exam. (c) Because of his absence at a workshop, he postpones a unit exam to permit more thorough discussion. (d) He distributes and discusses exam questions at the beginning of each unit, to direct student learning and to focus preparation. (e) He encourages students to raise questions about unclear governmental principles, and regularly pauses between sections in a presentation or discussion to allow time for these questions. (f) Outside of class time, he confers with students about their work. These Thursday help sessions are announced in his course description and reiterated each week. (g) Like Bob, he corrects inappropriate behavior by inserting names of inattentive students into his presentation and corrects student dress in his opening banter. Participants in Langdon's debate are sustained by information and plans for action.

Linda manages the literary journey through six strategies that encourage diligence and provide encouragement. (a) To prepare students for rapid analysis and the AP exam, she begins with a group-designed response to one question. Then in five stages, each requiring more independent thought and more restricted time than the last, students become familiar with and expert at the task. (b) She checks and approves thesis statements before the development of analytical essays. (c) She supplies the standards for judging the Lear essays—the importance of the thesis, the format, the value, and the form for quotations. (d) She responds to student inquiry, even when extraneous, before returning to the topic. (e) She provides opportunities for peer assistance. Linda sets aside time for partners to proofread and edit completed essays. (f) She meets with students outside of class time—before school, at noon, and after school—to discuss essay development. Linda values challenging journeys pursued systematically. She supports this work through carefully sequenced tasks and through cooperative assistance.

In managing the magic of physics, Conrad uses six strategies to promote critical thinking. (a) Because physics exam questions are interconnected, Conrad "sells" individual answers during tests in return for a lowered score. These purchased answers permit students to respond to more questions. He also arranges to confer with students outside of class time. (b) In discussion, he directs his questions toward the focus of a problem: "What do you need to know?" "How do you get that?" On unit exams he phrases questions to correspond to formulas emphasized in discussion. (c) He arranges activities to inform students immediately of their success. He dictates answers as problem sets are assigned so students can check their formulas immediately. (d) He pointedly reprimands student behavior that ignores earlier warnings. (e) He supports independent thought in discussion by encouraging student initiation even when nongermane; hypothesizing is especially rewarded. (f) Finally, he supports cooperative learning by encouraging students to help each other on problem sets. Because Conrad's organizing imagery is drawn from his understanding of student learning, it tends to provide greater influence on the conventional strategies rather than on these classroom mores. Instead of entertainment, this configuration values hard work, persistence, and imaginative thinking.

Important as the shared conventional and unique nature of these organizational strategies is, a much more salient feature of these classrooms is the sustained intellectual challenge of student work. These strategies regularly and consistently organize and support the independent thinking required of students. Some divide academic tasks into component parts. Others motivate students, gather knowledge, assess knowledge, provide information, or provide practice. Only on two occasions did I observe a higher order thinking task transformed into a lower order task by one of these strategies: once when Bob's model outline was taken to be a formula for a letter writing assignment, and once when Langdon provided the rubric for a unit exam question. Through negotiating and establishing classroom mores, Bob, Langdon, Linda, and Conrad, have maintained standards for critical thinking despite the daily press to reduce student anxiety.

6

Teaching Critical Thinking as a Cognitive Act

As described in preceding chapters, teaching critical thinking is a cognitive activity. It is a process that draws upon teacher knowledge in communicating subject matter to students. During these interactions with students, teachers accumulate facts and interpretations about content, pedagogy, students, and themselves that provide new comprehension for their knowledge base. Underlying this view of teaching is the notion that teachers directly influence the activities in the classroom but only indirectly influence students' learning. They provide learning opportunities for students, but learning and understanding occur only as a result of students' active participation in classroom activities (Bromme, 1987).

Moreover, it is clear from this study of four experienced teachers that the translation of higher order processing goals into instruction is challenging cognitive work. It requires broad and deep knowledge of subject matter. It requires viewing learning from a student work perspective. It requires understanding the social context of reasoning tasks and its management demands. It requires classroom mores that support intellectual risk-taking without diluting the task. From the wisdom of practice of these experienced teachers, we better understand the richness of classroom interactions and the intellectual activities that inform them.

KNOWLEDGE BASE FOR TEACHING CRITICAL THINKING

In the course of this book, I have documented the complexity associated with teaching critical thinking by focusing upon two important elements: what teachers must know and do in order to teach critical thinking, and

Figure 6–1
Knowledge Base for Teaching Critical Thinking: A Conceptual Model

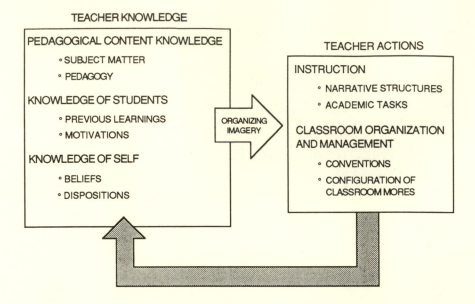

how these various kinds of knowledge relate to each other. These teaching documents reveal a knowledge base for teaching critical thinking that is divided into two major sections: teacher knowledge, which underlies planning lessons and preparing materials, and teacher actions, which make public this information during interactive teaching. These two sections are composed of five elements, which exert a recursive influence on each other: pedagogical content knowledge, knowledge of students, knowledge of self, instruction, and classroom organization and management. Together they represent the key elements used in teaching critical thinking (Figure 6–1).

Pedagogical content knowledge is that special combination of subject matter and pedagogy necessary for teaching. Borne of an in-depth study of a subject field, it structures an understanding of the nature of subject matter and the understanding of how one verifies or produces knowledge in that discipline. In their explanation of goals, each of these four teachers stresses fundamental concepts of his or her own dicipline: power in history, citizenship in government, critical theory in English, and matter and energy in physics. The four teachers also emphasize cognitive processes important to an understanding of that subject matter—writing, reading, and problem solving. But pedagogical content knowledge goes beyond a deep and abiding understanding of subject matter. It also includes knowing how to communicate that content to those who are less informed. This pedagogy specific to content involves understanding appropriate activities and tasks that provide opportunities for learning these concepts; it includes a repertoire of examples, metaphors, and analogies useful in communicating this content. To bring historical issues to life, for example, Bob uses comparisons drawn from sports and recreation; Langdon debates issues of political ideology; Linda coaches students in their individual struggles with literary analysis; and Conrad uses demonstration to illustrate the magic of physics. These activities communicate essential concepts from each teacher's conception of subject matter.

Knowledge of students is an understanding of those learner characteristics that influence learning. It involves an understanding of where students will have difficulty in learning these concepts and what misunderstandings or previous learning they may bring to the lesson. Bob and Langdon emphasize the conflict in historical and political events because their students assume important decisions to have been made easily; Linda warns her students about the necessary tedium in some parts of literary study and explains cultural interferences to her second-language students; and Conrad carefully distinguishes between color in light and color in pigment. Knowledge of students also includes an understanding of what motivates students to learn, both individually and as a group. With a highly verbal group, Bob paces the lesson rapidly, even though a quick pace is too fast for a few students; Langdon teases students to show interest in them as individuals in his classroom; Linda confronts her honors students' intolerance of diversity; and Conrad, believing that students find high school boring, mesmerizes through magical entertainment. This understanding of students influences the choice of activity and subject matter emphasis during teaching.

Knowledge of self includes teacher beliefs about what good teaching is and personal dispositions toward activities and interactions. Bob is comfortable in an active, energetic classroom where most students participate; he believes that education is fundamentally about learning to think about something. Langdon stresses highly informed and logical debate; like his personal demeanor, his classroom style is organized, controlled, and direct. Linda believes in reading for the pleasure of words, for literature's intrinsic value rather than for its utility; she also believes that learning is demanding work. And Conrad shares parts of his personal life with his students in return for their participation; his close relation with students is based on personal appeal. These beliefs, principles, and interests also interact with the content and pedagogy, shaping this knowledge in plans and materials.

This knowledge is mediated through an *organizing imagery* that transforms knowledge of content, pedagogy, students, and self into action. These four teachers make sense of their reality by using this meta-image as a controlling conception for planning, implementing, and managing curriculum activities. It is a frame or way of looking at things and a process by which new understandings come into existence. For Bob, the game of history has rules of conduct that operate within constricted boundaries. Within this context, there are sometimes referees who judge action and assess penalties. For Langdon, the political battle presents opposing viewpoints contesting for the supremacy of one. There are, therefore, winners and losers. Linda's literary journey imagery carries linearity; pilgrimages have beginnings, middles, and ends. They also carry a temporality, and there is a self-contained-ness for each segment on the way. Finally, Conrad's magic of Physics–land is an alternative to the conventional. It asks a suspension of normal rules as counterintuitive events occur. With magic, things one does not expect to happen happen, and one has to be alert for the unexpected; this attention gives pure pleasure. It also bestows power to those who possess it.

The selection of an effective organizing imagery, a single metaphor to represent a complex process, is not easy. Its usefulness in providing coherence for teacher actions appears to be related to its source in teacher knowledge. At least in this study, those teachers who selected an organizing imagery from their understanding of subject matter and pedagogy found more coherence in their classroom actions. The game, for example, drawn from an understanding of power in historical events, also influences the explanation of content, the design of academic tasks, and the selection of pedagogy. The one teacher who drew an image from conceptions other than subject matter or pedagogy provided less coherence in classroom actions. Magic, drawn from an understanding of student motivation, colors explanation and demonstrations but does not influence the design of academic tasks or their organization. In fact, it sometimes interferes with the management of those tasks by appearing as entertainment rather than work. If teachers with relatively weaker pedagogical content knowledge select images from other segments of their knowledge that are more fully developed, as Conrad did, they may both misrepresent content understandings for students and undermine their own valiant efforts to sustain student participation.

Instruction, one of two kinds of teacher actions, is the means for making public the teacher's content knowledge and for transforming this understanding into student performance. These four teachers use narrative structures as explanation to unfold their subject matter knowledge and pedagogical thinking. This explanation takes on a variety of forms of representation, from concrete to abstract, which makes public content information for students. Coach Bob uses chalkboard outlines of extended definitions for historical events; Langdon maps a mathematical model for predicting political party factions; Linda provides a reading guide for *The Bear*; and Conrad uses physical models to illustrate the lens property of the cornea. The thinking that students are expected to perform, however, is contained not in these explanations but in assigned academic tasks. In Bob's classroom, the history game requires students to compare the impact of the Stamp Act on competing groups; in Langdon's classroom, the battle focuses essay questions upon the contrasting views of the political right and left; in Linda's classroom, the journey of literary analysis contains periods of attention to the detail of punctuation rules intersected by opportunities for reading great sweeps of literature; in Conrad's classroom, critical thinking tasks such as tests or problem sets are direct and straightforward, relatively untouched by magic. Students in these classrooms understand the meaning of history, government, literature, and physics as the work performed in these academic tasks.

Strategies for *classroom organization and management* in teaching critical thinking, a second component of teacher actions, create classroom environments that support intellectual risk-taking. These strategies, which monitor and sustain participation in group activities, include both classroom conventions and configurations of classroom mores. These strategies are particularly important in teaching critical thinking because they manage the press between demands for student self-direction and a teacher's learning goals. During higher order thinking tasks, this press is increased as the intellectual space berween the known and the novel increases and as evaluation criteria become more ambiguous. Six strategies appeared in all classrooms in this study, regardless of subject matter content or academic tasks: using writing to learn, discussing major topics thoroughly, interjecting humor to lighten otherwise serious work, responding supportively to student comments, ignoring incongruous student responses, and correcting erroneous thinking. These appear to be traditional patterns of organizational behavior for all teachers. In addition to these conventions, each of the four teachers selected a group of five to seven classroom mores with which to build community and establish shared classroom values. In Bob's game plan, historical tasks are maintained by modeling effective performance, using peer support, distributing essay questions prior to testing, altering deadlines to allow adequate preparation, and correcting inappropriate behavior. Langdon organizes his students for political battles through providing immediate feedback, clarifying expectations for final products, altering deadlines to allow adequate preparation, distributing essay questions prior to testing, soliciting student questions, providing individual assistance to students, and correcting inappropriate behavior. Linda guides her students through literary journeys by sequencing a series of activities to move from the known to the unknown, using progress checks at key intervals in a major task, clarifying expectations for final products, providing immediate feedback, using peer support, and providing individual assistance to students. Finally, Conrad motivates students through the magic of physics: providing individual assistance to students, phrasing questions to clarify thinking and build confidence, providing immediate feedback, correcting inappropriate behavior, soliciting student questions, and using peer support. These strategies function on several levels. Some serve to divide academic tasks into component parts; others motivate students, provide information or practice, or assess knowledge. They maintain the intellectual challenge of academic tasks.

The relation between a teacher's instruction and classroom organization and management is interactive. The nature of the academic tasks assigned influences a teacher's management task: Structural features of critical thinking tasks, because of their greater ambiguity and risk, require varied, complex, and sustained monitoring. Conversely, a teacher's management system, by its emphasis on predictable routine, may also preclude the inclusion of critical thinking tasks. An emphasis on quiet, orderly classrooms does not permit the discussion needed to synthesize ideas. In addition, teachers of critical thinking must recognize students' press for predictability and order as inherent to academic tasks, rather than as a feature of poor communication. Without this understanding, they are likely to reduce unknowingly the cognitive challenge of the task. If, for example, a teacher's management behaviors reduce the intellectual challenge of a task—if they transform a reasoning task into a memory task—the nature of what is learned during instruction is changed. The balance in this reciprocal tension between organizational and instructional processes thus has a direct effect on what students learn.

Finally, information learned during classroom instruction and organization, particularly knowledge about students' motivations and previous learnings and about the relative success of pedagogical strategies, influences teacher knowledge. In reflective teachers, this new information alters and reorganizes existing knowledge, thereby enriching their understanding. This evolving theory of teachers as knowledgeable practitioners describes how teachers, working in a supportive setting, select, modify, and adapt content in teaching critical thinking.

This conceptual model of the knowledge base for teaching critical thinking advances our understanding of cognition in teaching in three important ways. First of all, it enriches our understanding of several components identified by Shulman (1987) by showing how four teachers enact in classrooms the content necessary for critical thinking. It also divides the knowledge base into teacher understanding and teacher actions in order to clarify the relations among its components. As such, its structure plays a useful "heuristic role" (Phillips, 1986, p. 12) in our developing understanding of the knowledge base for teaching critical thinking. Second, this framework suggests that teacher knowledge is mediated through an organizing imagery into teacher actions. The wisdom of practice shows that able teachers use this image to fuse the multiple processes in the highly complex task of teaching. The strength of this cohesion, however, depends upon the selection of an image that is particularly useful in communicating subject matter. Third, these case studies also point to one dimension missing from the existing framework—namely, knowledge of self—which influences teacher knowledge in important ways. Because each of these four teachers believes that an educated person is one who can think critically about domain-specific knowledge, each stresses major concepts and cognitive strategies necessary to understand those concepts. Further, their personal dispositions restructure and coordinate content. Bob's participation in educational policy as a school board member and Langdon's legal experiences influence the selection of their organizing metaphor. Linda's dispositions toward fairness and individuals sometimes conflict in the classroom, especially when deciding when an essay is submitted on time. And Conrad's view that all students perceive classroom activities as he did as a student has shaped his controlling imagery and classroom performance.

Neither this framework nor the case studies from which it is derived, however, explain how this knowledge base develops, whether individual elements are stable or evolving, or how external constraints such as time or felt responsibility to students influence this knowledge. Instead, like all conceptual frameworks, this one serves three functions (Byrne, 1983): It clearly displays the focus of attention in this study; it sets out relations among concepts; and it directs attention to gaps in this knowledge that are pertinent to further study.

IMPLICATIONS FOR TEACHING AND TEACHER EDUCATION

Nonetheless, the research described here may have important implications for teaching and teacher education. Although I am uncertain about how this knowledge base develops, I do know that these teachers had difficulty in explaining how they use it; they possess an educational and moral language for explaining only part of the thinking in their cognitive work as teachers. Like the experienced high school social studies teachers in Peterson and Comeaux's study (1987), these teachers could articulate with elaboration and detail which activities they chose to teach or why they chose to intervene in managing student behavior, but they had difficulty in explaining the richness of understanding used when anticipating students' misconceptions of a concept or when selecting one concept instead of another. Teacher statements, at least as represented by the four experienced teachers in this study, reveal a meager vocabulary for discussing this knowledge: Their conceptions of pedagogical knowledge, knowledge of self, and knowledge of students are blurred and fuzzy. As a result, teacher knowledge is missing not only from research on teaching, as Shulman (1986a) has suggested; it is also missing from the language used by teachers in communicating the reasoning of their professional decisions and actions.

As educators, we can strengthen the conception of teaching as cognitive work by introducing the components of teacher knowledge into our professional language. There is recent precedent for just this kind of language change. Prior to the introduction of the concept of academic learning time (Denham and Lieberman, 1980), few teachers thought of time as a precious classroom commodity; today, many can discuss the components of academic learning time as well as its relation to learning. A similar conceptual shift is needed to make possible discourse on the content base for teaching. As educators, we can also regularly and systematically invite teachers to articulate their conceptions of subject matter as a part of their education and their professional work.

This study, in deepening our understanding of how able practitioners teach critical thinking, has identified a second characteristic problem in our educational tradition, a meager training model for developing the knowledge base for teaching. Our understanding of the complexities of this knowledge base may restructure our conceptions of professional education. At the present time, teacher educators assume that beginning teachers, with experience, will develop the sophisticated knowledge that experienced teachers presently have. But it is incorrect to assume that simply giving teachers information on the knowledge base for teaching critical thinking and time in classrooms will automatically strengthen their domain-specific knowledge and transform them into teachers of critical thinking. Such an assumption oversimplifies the complex process these four teachers have gone through to develop their knowledge base. Rather than leaving the beginning teacher to learn through trial and error, professional education must be redesigned with greater emphasis on subject matter understanding and how that subject matter is explained to students—in short, with greater emphasis on reflective, critical thinking about teaching. Moreover, we need to fuse pre-service and in-service education in ways that will permit this knowledge base to develop through the early years of a teaching career. Further study on how this knowledge base develops may contribute training models for this intervention. Our goal is teachers with the habits of mind for teaching critical thinking.

References

Anderson, L., Evertson, C., and Emmer, E. (1982). Dimensions of classroom management derived from recent research. *Journal of Curriculum Studies, 12*, 343–356.

Applebee, A. (1981). *Writing in the secondary school: English and the content areas.* Urbana, IL: National Council of Teachers of English.

————. (1984). Writing and reasoning. *Review of Educational Research, 54*, 577–596.

Arendt, H. (1977, November 28). Reflections: Thinking (II). *The New Yorker*, pp. 114–164.

Association for Supervision and Curriculum Development. (1985). *Resolutions 1985.* Arlington, VA: author.

Bailey, T., and Kennedy, D. (1983). *Teachers' manual for American pageant* (7th ed.). New York: D. C. Heath.

Barzun, J. (1981). *Teacher in America.* Indianapolis: Liberty Press. (Original work published in 1945.)

Baxter, J., Richert, A., and Saylor, C. (1985, April). *Science group: Content and process of biology.* Paper presented at the meeting of the American Educational Research Association, Chicago.

Boyer, E. (1983). *High school: A report on secondary education in America.* Princeton, NJ: Carnegie Foundation for the Advancement of Teaching.

Bromme, R. (1987). Teachers' assessments of students' difficulties and progress in understanding the classroom. In J. Calderhead (Ed.), *Exploring teachers' thinking* (pp. 125–146). London: Cassell.

Brophy, J. (1983). Classroom organization and management. *The Elementary School Journal, 83*, 265–285.

Brophy, J., and Putnam, J. (1978). *Classroom management in the elementary grades* (Research Series no. 32). East Lansing: Michigan State University, Institute for Research on Teaching.

Brown, J. (1983). On teaching thinking skills in the elementary and middle school. *Phi Delta Kappan, 64,* 709–714.

Bruner, J. (1971). *Toward a theory of instruction.* Cambridge: Belknap Press of Harvard University Press.

Byrne, C. (1983, October). *Teacher knowledge and teacher effectiveness: A literature review, theoretical analysis and discussion of research strategy.* Paper presented at the 14th Convocation of the Northeastern Research Association, Ellenville, NY.

Calderhead, J. (1986, April). *Developing a framework for the elicitation and analysis of teachers' verbal reports.* Paper presented at the meeting of the American Educational Research Association, San Francisco.

Calfee, R. (1981). Cognitive psychology and educational practice. In D. Berliner (Ed.), *Review of research in education,* Vol. 9 (pp. 3–74). Washington, DC: American Educational Research Association.

_____. (1986, April). *Explicitness characterizes good teaching.* Paper presented at the meeting of the American Educational Research Association, San Francisco.

Carnegie Task Force on Teaching as a Profession. (1986). *A nation prepared: Teachers for the 21st century.* Washington, DC: Carnegie Forum on Education and the Economy.

Carter, K. (1986, April). *Classroom management as cognitive problem solving: Toward teacher comprehension in teacher education.* Paper presented at the meeting of the American Educational Research Association, San Francisco.

Chesterton, G. K. (1957). The logic of elfland. In M. Gardner (Ed.), *Great essays in science* (pp. 77–83). New York: Pocket Library.

Clandinin, D. (1985). Personal practical knowledge: A study of teachers' classroom images. *Curriculum Inquiry, 15,* 361–385.

_____. (1986). *Classroom practice: Teacher images in action.* Philadelphia: The Falmer Press.

Clark, C., and Lampert, M. (1985, April). *What knowledge is of most worth to teachers: Insights from studies of teacher thinking.* Paper presented at the meeting of the American Educational Research Association, Chicago, IL.

Clark, C., and Peterson, P. (1986). Teachers' thought processes. In M. Wittrock (Ed.), *Handbook of research on teaching,* 3rd ed. (pp. 255–296). New York: Macmillan.

Clifford, G. (1984). Buch un lessen: Historical perspectives on literacy and schooling. *Review of Educational Research, 54,* 472–500.

Clift, R., and Morgan, P. (1986, April). *Future English teacher or English major? Exploring qualitative differences in subject matter knowledge.* Paper presented at the meeting of the American Educational Research Association, San Francisco.

Commons, D. (1985). *Who will teach our children? A strategy for improving California's schools.* Sacramento: California Commission on the Teaching Profession.

Computers can help kids learn to think. (1985, Spring). *Wisconsin Center for Educational Research News,* pp. 3, 12.

Confrey, J. (1982). Content and pedagogy in secondary schools. *Journal of Teacher Education, 33,* 13–16.

Connelly, F., and Clandinin, D. (1985) Personal practical knowledge and the modes of knowing: Relevance for teaching and learning. In E. Eisner (Ed.), *Learning and teaching: The ways of knowing* (pp. 174–198). Eighty-fourth Yearbook of the National Society for the Study of Education, Part II. Chicago: The University of Chicago Press.

Costa, A. (n.d.). *Teaching for intelligent behavior*. Mimeographed.

Cuban, L. (1984). Policy and research dilemmas in the teaching of reasoning: Unplanned designs. *Review of Educational Research, 54*, 655–681.

Cusick, P. (1973). *Inside high school: The students' world*. New York: Holt, Rinehart and Winston.

Dawes, H. (1984). Teaching: A performing art. *Phi Delta Kappan, 65*, 548–552.

de Bono, E. (1983). The direct teaching of thinking as a skill. *Phi Delta Kappan, 64*, 703–707.

Denham, C., and Lieberman, A. (Eds.) (1980). *Time to learn*. Washington, DC: National Institute of Education.

Dillard, J. (1987, April). *Getting into the bargain: A study of teacher interactional thinking and improvisation*. Paper presented at the meeting of the American Educational Research Association, Washington, DC.

Doyle, W. (1977). Paradigms for research on teacher effectiveness. In L. Shulman (Ed.), *Review of research in education*, Vol. 5 (pp. 163–198). Itasca, IL: Peacock.

————. (1979a). Making managerial decisions in classrooms. In D. Duke (Ed.), *Classroom management* (pp. 42–74). Seventy-eighth Yearbook of the National Society for the Study of Education, Part II. Chicago: The University of Chicago Press.

————. (1979b). *The tasks of teaching and learning in classrooms* (R & D Report 4103). Austin: The University of Texas, Research and Development Center for Teacher Education.

————. (1983). Academic work. *Review of Educational Research, 53*, 159–199.

————. (1984a). *Effective classroom practices for secondary schools* (R & D Report 6191). Austin: The University of Texas, Research and Development Center for Teacher Education.

————. (1985). *Content representation in teachers' definitions of academic work* (R & D Report 6161). Austin: The University of Texas, Research and Development Center for Teacher Education.

————. (1986). Classroom organization and management. In M. Wittrock (Ed.), *Handbook of research on teaching*, 3rd ed. (pp. 392–431). New York: Macmillan.

Doyle, W., and Carter, K. (1984). Academic tasks in classrooms. *Curriculum Inquiry, 14*, 139–149.

————. (1987). Choosing the means of instruction. In V. Richardson-Koehler (Ed.), *Educator's handbook: A research perspective* (pp. 188–206). New York: Longman.

Doyle, W., Sanford, J., Clements, B., Schmidt French, B., and Emmer, E. (1983). *Managing academic tasks: An interim report of the junior high school study* (R & D Report 6186). Austin: The University of Texas, Research and Development Center for Teacher Education.

Eisner, E. (1982). *Cognition and curriculum: A basis for deciding what to teach*. New York: Longman.

————. (1985). *The educational imagination: On the design and evaluation of school programs*, 2nd ed. New York: Macmillan.

Elbaz, F. (1983). *Teacher thinking: A study of practical knowledge.* New York: Nichols.

Erickson, F. (1972). *What makes school ethnography "ethnographic"?* Report to participants in an American Educational Research Association Training Workshop. (ERIC Document Reproduction Service No. ED 093 726.)

Feiman-Nemser, S. (1983). Learning to teach. In L. Shulman and G. Sykes (Eds.), *Handbook of teaching and policy* (pp. 150–170). New York: Longman.

————. (1987, April 15). Personal correspondence.

Feiman-Nemser, S., and Buchmann, M. (1986). The first year of teacher preparation: Transition to pedagogical thinking? *Journal of Curriculum Studies, 18,* 239–256.

Feiman-Nemser, S., and Floden, F. (1986). The cultures of teaching. In M. Wittrock (Ed.), *Handbook of research on teaching,* 3rd ed. (pp. 505–526). New York: Macmillan.

Fenstermacher, G. (1978). A philosophical consideration of recent research on teacher effectiveness. In L. Shulman (Ed.), *Review of research in education,* Vol. 6 (pp. 157–185). Itasca, IL: Peacock.

Forbes, R., and Brown, R. (1981). *Reading, thinking, and writing.* Denver: National Assessment of Educational Progress.

Frederiksen, C., and Dominic, J. (1981). *Writing: The nature, development, and teaching of written composition,* Vol. II. Hillsdale, NJ: Erlbaum.

Frederiksen, N. (1984). Implications of cognitive theory for instruction in problem-solving. *Review of Educational Research, 54,* 363–408.

Gage, N. (1978). *The scientific basis of the art of teaching.* New York: Teachers College Press.

Glaser, B., and Strauss, A. (1967). *The discovery of grounded theory: Strategies for qualitative research.* New York: Aldine.

Glasman, N., Koff, R., and Spiers, H. (1984). Preface. *Review of Educational Research, 54,* 461–471.

Goodlad, J. (1983). *A place called school: Prospects for the future.* New York: McGraw-Hill.

Grossman, P., Reynolds, A., Ringstaff, C., and Sykes, G. (1985, April). *English major to English teacher: New approaches to an old problem.* Paper presented at the meeting of the American Educational Research Association, Chicago.

Gudmundsdottir, S. (1987a, April). *Learning to teach social studies: Case studies of Chris and Cathy.* Paper presented at the meeting of the American Educational Research Association, Washington, DC.

————. (1987b, April). *Pedagogical content knowledge: Teachers' ways of knowing.* Paper presented at the meeting of the American Educational Research Association, Washington, DC.

Gudmundsdottir, S., Carey, N., and Wilson, S. (1985, April). *Role of prior subject matter knowledge in learning to teach social studies.* Paper presented at the meeting of the American Educational Research Association, Chicago.

Haney, W. (1984). Testing reasoning and reasoning about testing. *Review of Educational Research, 54,* 597–654.

Hazlett, S. (1987, April). *Facets of history.* Paper presented at the meeting of the American Educational Research Association, Washington, DC.

Holton, G. (1984). Metaphors in science and education. In W. Taylor (Ed.), *Metaphors of education* (pp. 91–113). London: Heinemann.

Jackson, P. (1968). *Life in classrooms*. New York: Holt, Rinehart and Winston.

Jones, R., and Wimmers, E. (n.d.). *Multiple-choice testing in literature: Advanced placement English*. Princeton, NJ: Advanced Placement Program of The College Board.

Karweit, N. (1983). *Time-on-task: A research review* (Report No. 332). Baltimore: The Johns Hopkins University, Center for Social Organization of Schools.

Keating, D. (1980). Four faces of creativity: The continuing plight of the intellectually underserved. *Gifted Child Quarterly, 24,* 56–61.

Kerr, D. (1983). Teaching competence and teacher education in the United States. In L. Shulman and G. Sykes (Eds.), *Handbook of teaching and policy* (pp. 126–149). New York: Longman.

Knitter, W. (1987, April). *Subject matter in a deliberative context.* Paper presented at the meeting of the American Educational Research Association, Washington, DC.

Kounin, J. (1970). *Discipline and group management in classrooms*. New York: Holt, Rinehart and Winston.

Lampert, M. (1985). How do teachers manage to teach? Perspectives on problems in practice. *Harvard Educational Review, 55,* 178–194.

Lanier, J. (1986) *Tomorrow's teachers: A report of the Holmes Group*. East Lansing: Michigan State University.

Leinhardt, G. (1986, April). *Math lessons: A contrast of novice and expert competence.* Paper presented at the meeting of the American Educational Research Association, San Francisco.

Mansfield, R., and Busse, T. (1982). Creativity. In H. Mitzel (Ed.), *Encyclopedia of Educational Research* (5th ed., pp. 385–394). New York: The Free Press.

Mansfield, R., Busse, T., and Krepelka, E. (1978). The effectiveness of creativity training. *Review of Educational Research, 48,* 517–536.

Mayer, R. (1975). Information processing variables in learning to solve problems. *Review of Educational Research, 45,* 525–541.

McPeck, J. (1981). *Critical thinking and education*. New York: St. Martin's Press.

Mitman, A., Mergendoller, J., Packer, J., and Marchman, V. (1984). *Scientific literacy in seventh-grade life science: A study of instructional process, task completion, student perceptions and learning outcomes.* San Francisco: Far West Laboratory for Educational Research and Development.

Morine-Dershimer, G. (1984, April). *Complexity and imagery in teacher thought: Alternative analyses of stimulated recall data.* Paper presented at the meeting of the American Educational Research Association, New Orleans.

Munby, H. (1985, April). *Teachers' professional knowledge: A study of metaphor.* Paper presented at the annual meeting of the American Educational Research Association, Chicago.

————. (1986). Metaphor in the thinking of teachers: An exploratory study. *Journal of Curriculum Studies, 18,* 197–209.

National Commission on Excellence in Education. (1983). *A nation at risk: The imperative for educational reform.* Washington, DC: U.S. Department of Education.

Nespor, J. (1987). Academic tasks in a high school English class. *Curriculum Inquiry, 17,* 203–228.

Noddings, N. (1984). *Caring: A feminine approach to ethics and moral education.* Berkeley: The University of California Press.

Peterson, P., and Comeaux, M. (1985, April). *Teachers' schemata for classroom events: The mental scaffolding of teachers' thinking during classroom instruction.* Paper presented at the meeting of the American Educational Research Association, Chicago.

Peterson, P., and Walberg, H. (Eds.). (1979). *Research on teaching.* Berkeley: McCutchan.

Phillips, D. (1986, April). *The conceptual minefield of structure: Mediations after studying the knowledge structures of student teachers.* Paper presented at the meeting of the American Educational Research Association, San Francisco.

Popham, J., and Baker, E. (1970). *Systematic instruction.* Englewood Cliffs, NJ: Prentice-Hall.

Reinharz, S. (1984). *On becoming a social scientist: From survey research and participant observation to experiential analysis* (2nd ed.). New Brunswick, NJ: Transaction Books.

Richardson-Koehler, V. (1987, April 14). Personal correspondence.

Rosenshine, B. (1983). Teaching functions in instructional programs. *The Elementary School Journal, 83,* 335–352.

Russell, T. (1986, April). *Beginning teachers' development of knowledge-in-action.* Paper presented at the meeting of the American Educational Research Association, San Francisco, CA.

————. (1987, April). *Learning the professional knowledge of teaching: Views of the relationship between theory and practice.* Paper presented at the meeting of the American Educational Research Association, Washington, DC.

Schon, D. (1979). Generative metaphor: A perspective on problem-solving in social policy. In A. Ortony (Ed.), *Metaphor and thought* (pp. 254–283). Cambridge: Cambridge University Press.

————. (1983). *The reflective practitioner.* New York: Basic Books.

Schwab, J. (1978a). Education and the structure of the disciplines. In I. Westbury and N. Wilkof (Eds.), *Science, curriculum and liberal education: Selected essays* (pp. 229–272). Chicago: The University of Chicago Press. (Original work written in 1961.)

————. (1978b). The practical: A language for curriculum. In I. Westbury and N. Wilkof (Eds.), *Science, curriculum and liberal education: Selected Essays* (pp. 287–321). Chicago: The University of Chicago Press. (Original work published in 1970.)

Shakespeare, W. (G. Kittredge, Ed.). (1940). *The tragedy of King Lear.* New York: Ginn.

Shavelson, R., and Dempsey-Atwood, N. (1976). Generalizability of measures of teaching behavior. *Review of Educational Research, 46,* 553–611.

Shavelson, R., and Stern, P. (1981). Research on teachers' pedagogical thoughts, judgments, decisions, and behavior. *Review of Educational Research, 51,* 455–498.

Shulman, L. (1974). The psychology of school subjects: A premature orbituary? *Journal of Research on Science Teaching, 11,* 319–339.

————. (1986a). Paradigms and research programs in the study of teaching. In

M. Wittrock (Ed.), *Handbook of research on teaching*, 3rd ed. (pp. 3–36). New York: Macmillan.

————. (1986b). Those who understand: Knowledge growth in teaching. *Educational Researcher, 15* (2), 4–14.

————. (1987). Knowledge and teaching: Foundations of the new reform. *Harvard Educational Review, 57*, 1–22.

Shulman, L., and Carey, N. (1984). Psychology and the limitations of individual rationality: Implications for the study of reasoning and civility. *Review of Educational Research, 54*, 501–524.

Shulman, L., Sykes, G., and Phillips, D. (1983, November). *Knowledge growth in a profession: The development of knowledge in teaching.* Proposal submitted to the Spencer Foundation. Stanford University School of Education.

Sizer, T. (1984). *Horace's compromise: The dilemma of the American high school.* Boston: Houghton Mifflin.

Smith, L., and Geoffrey, W. (1968). *The complexities of the urban classroom.* New York: Holt, Rinehart and Winston.

Smith, S. (1983). *Improving the attractiveness of the k–12 teaching profession in California.* Sacramento: The California Round Table on Educational Opportunity.

Sockett, H. (1987). Has Shulman got the strategy right? *Harvard Educational Review, 57*, 208–219.

Stallings, J. (1980). Allocated academic learning time revisited, or beyond time on task. *Educational Researcher, 9*(11), 11–16.

Stewart, R., and Bethurum, D. (Eds.). (1954). *Modern American narration: Mark Twain, Ernest Hemingway, William Faulkner.* Glenview, IL: Scott, Foresman.

Sykes, G. (1985, March). *Teaching higher order cognitive skills in today's classrooms: An exploration of some problems.* Testimony presented to the California Commission on the Teaching Profession, Claremont.

Tamir, P. (1987, April). *Subject matter and related pedagogical knowledge in teacher education.* Paper presented at the annual meeting of the American Educational Research Association, Washington, DC.

Tyler, R. (1949). *Basic principles of curriculum and instruction.* Chicago: The University of Chicago Press.

Wagner, R., and Sternberg R. (1984). Alternative conceptions of intelligence and their implications for education. *Review of Educational Research, 54*, 179–224.

Williams, J , Trinklein, F., Metcalfe, H., and Lefler, R. (1972). *Modern physics.* New York: Holt, Rinehart and Winston.

Wilson, S., and Gudmundsdottir, S. (1986, April). *Perennial problems in qualitative research: What is this a case of?* Paper presented at the meeting of the American Educational Research Association, San Francisco.

Wilson, S., and Wineburg, S. (1987, April). *Peering at history through different lenses: The role of disciplinary perspectives in the teaching of American History.* Paper presented at the meeting of the American Educational Research Association, Washington, DC.

Yinger, R. (1986, April). *Examining thought in action: A theoretical and methodological critique of research on interactive teaching.* Paper presented at the meeting of the American Educational Research Association, San Francisco.

Index

About the Author

GRACE E. GRANT is Associate Professor of Education at Occidental College in Los Angeles. In education for more than 20 years, she began her career as a high school English teacher; later she obtained a Ph.D. from The Claremont Graduate School. She currently directs a professional education program for elementary and secondary teaching candidates. Since joining Occidental, her research and publications have focused on the teaching-learning process and the ways it might be appropriately understood, appraised, and improved. She is a contributing author to *Studies in College Teaching*, and initiated this study while a John D. MacArthur Research Professor at Occidental in 1984.